THE
SCHOOL
OF
DYING
GRACES

The School of

Lessons on living
from two extraordinary
journeys toward God

Dying Graces

RICHARD FELIX

WITH ROB WILKINS

SALT**RIVER**™

AN IMPRINT OF
TYNDALE HOUSE PUBLISHERS, INC.

Visit Tyndale's exciting Web site at www.tyndale.com

Designed by Beth Sparkman

Library of Congress Cataloging-in-Publication Data

Felix, Richard, date.
    The school of dying graces : a journey of extraordinary intimacy with God / Richard Felix with Rob Wilkins.
        p. cm.
    ISBN 1-4143-0066-2 (hardcover)
    1. Felix, Vivian, d. date. 2. Breast—Cancer—Patients—Religious life. 3. Terminally ill—Religious life. 4. Felix, Richard, date. I. Wilkins, Rob. II. Title.
    BV4910.33.F45 2004
    248.8'66'092—dc22   2004006000

DEDICATION

*This book for the ages
belongs to Vivian's children:
Doak David,
Tristram Earl,
and Melissa Elizabeth Marshall;
to those precious grandchildren,
Tatum Grace Marshall,
Jackson Earl Felix,
and Collier Doak Marshall,
and to all our future grandchildren.*

ChristianBookGuides.com

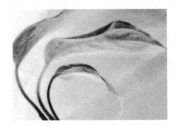

SaltRiver Books are a bit like saltwater: buoyant; sometimes stinging; a mixture of sweet and bitter, just like real life. These books are intelligent, thoughtful, and finely crafted—but not pretentious, condescending, or out of reach. They take on real life from a Christian perspective. Look for SaltRiver Books, an imprint of Tyndale House Publishers, everywhere Christian books are sold.

SALTRIVER™

CONTENTS

THE GRACE OF TRANSFORMATION

FOREWORD
by
Richard Foster

The School of Dying Graces is a beautiful book. I do not say this lightly. When Richard Felix sat on our deck a few weeks after Vivian's death and told me of his desire to collect some of her journal notations into book form, I could indeed see a book: a tragic book, a sad book, a consoling book, perhaps even a hopeful book . . . but certainly not a beautiful book. The circumstances were too crushing, the end too tragic for anything like beauty to be connected with it. But I was wrong. This book *is* beautiful . . . beautiful and graceful and charming and inviting—just like the woman whose story it tells.

I have known Richard and Vivian for more than two decades. Both of our families came to Friends University in the same year: Richard as university president and I as a professor and writer-in-residence. Quickly our lives were intertwined, not just professionally but as friends. Both couples—Richard and Vivian and Carolynn and I—had young children who sometimes played together at backyard barbeques. Vivian and Carolynn were part of a small friendship group of women at the university who gathered informally to celebrate one another's birthdays and sometimes to plan more formal university-related events. One year our two families had Thanksgiving dinner together, all exquisitely prepared and served by Vivian. Our friendship continued unabated when Richard accepted the presidency of Azusa Pacific University, for he graciously invited me to teach there regularly.

But friendship does not a book make! Not to mention a book of surpassing beauty. So, what is it that makes this story so compelling, so gripping, so beautiful? Three things.

First, the story is told well. This comes supremely from the hand of Vivian Felix herself. I have long known of Vivian's skill with the English language—she was, after all, an English teacher. Years back I invited her to be part of a small group of critical readers for my own writings-in-progress; I chose Vivian precisely for her facility with language. But, I had no idea . . . these journal writings, penned under the white-hot heat of suffering and brokenness and loss, are simply stunning. The words are well chosen and the images are memorable. Combined with a vulnerability that takes your breath away, these words produce a heart-language that is radiant. Such beauty always has a way of touching the subterranean sanctuary of our soul, and somehow even while detailing the deepest of anguish, it lifts us up into the good, the true, the beautiful. Listen to her words: "As I was praying I visualized my heart and on the left lower side there was a wound. As I watched it, the wound festered and came to a head. A tumor came out of it, fell, and was planted in the soil. After a while, a plant grew up and blossomed. I was left with the picture of a single green plant with a single stalk and, at the top, a lovely heart-shaped flower."

Second, the story is told with brutal honesty. Richard should be commended here, for he refuses to hide from us the awful savagery of "the Beast," as Vivian dubbed her particularly virulent form of can-

x

cer. In heartrending detail this book is an extended commentary on those poignant lines at the end of Shakespeare's *King Lear:* "The weight of this sad time we must obey, / Speak what we feel, not what we ought to say." It is sad indeed, this telling of the wasting away of one so lovely and so vibrant. And yet, as Richard obeys the sad time and speaks to us, not in pious platitudes, but in the stark realities of pain and sadness and anguish, we are slowly, almost imperceptibly, changed for the good. It is as if we are being immersed into the fiery baptism of Richard and Vivian's suffering and somehow—I don't know how—we emerge better, nobler, stronger.

Third, it is the story of a beautiful soul. To become beautiful of soul is perhaps the greatest grace of all, and in a way deeper and fuller than most of us, Vivian Felix entered into this grace. How suffering purifies! From the defining vision she received at England's Warwick Castle, to the tearful clinging to a rough wooden cross at Mission La Purísima Concepción, to the divine refrain "Trust me" spoken to her, to her determined decision to "enter the school of dying graces," to her quiet query to her husband, "Dare we imagine what it will be like to see each other in heaven?" Vivian grew in grace. Immeasurably so.

This is an important book, because in the midst of our death-denying culture, it is good to realize that dying well has a beauty all its own. "Precious in the sight of the Lord is the death of his saints" (Psalm 116:15).

Robert Frost wrote:

> *Two roads diverged in a wood, and I—*
> *I took the one less traveled by,*
> *And that has made all the difference.*

With faith and courage, Vivian Felix chose to take the road less traveled. Through the pages of this book, we can travel down that road with her.

—Richard J. Foster

FOREWORD
by
Jack Hayford

It's my privilege to introduce this deeply moving, thought-trans-
forming book—one that centers on two friends of mine, but also
relates to two words, words that summarize the conflict they faced.
As you will find, the conflict wasn't between my friends, for theirs
was a profound partnership. Rather, the conflict they resolved and
dominated was an ever-present battle between two words that are
acute enemies.

Let me explain.

As a communicator, I've learned to read the faces of people and
groups, to sense moods, to perceive the human response or the
"spirit" awakened when certain words or ideas are spoken.
Whether in private discussion or during a platform address, a no-
ticeable reaction occurs when the word *hope* is even uttered. That
is, of course, when the hearers recognize you are referencing that
quality of hope that transcends the casual or the pop notions
"Cross your fingers and . . ." or "Well, I guess we can take another
shot and 'hope for the best.'"

Hope, in this instance, is infinitely more. Genuine hope is a substance, not a superstition—a reality, not a ruse. When its substance and reality are communicated—and they are, on this book's

pages—hope has a way of infusing strength, undergirding comfort, transforming faith, and begetting profound durability. And hope abounds here, in this remarkably dynamic testament to one couple's experience facing a ferocious enemy's assault. That enemy was cancer—the other word prompting my reflection.

As a pastor-counselor, I've found no greater opponent to hope than cancer. Spoken, the very word blackens horizons and dissipates hope like twilight before midnight. How often I've observed it—once spoken, the word *cancer* dropping an icy weight into the soul, crushing the spirit like a lead glacier. Hope is hard to conjure when cancer is mentioned; the word itself becomes toxic. Once declared in diagnosis, it seems to emit an acrid atmosphere—a sinister presence that ensconces fear, dares faith to lift its head, and drains hope from a soul just as disease drains health from a body.

But I turn from my reflection, for this introduction is not about a poetic analysis of words, but rather an effort at giving a context for my belief in this book's message . . . and my privilege in knowing the two people central to its story. I see *The School of Dying Graces* as a weapon against anything that assails hope, as a source of nourishing hope's substance in anyone's soul. Not only is this a true story, it's a truth story: a message of vital life, even when facing death—an avenue to the power to rise up, even when circumstance puts you down.

In this book, you will meet two profoundly loving people: the author, Richard Felix, former president of Azusa Pacific University, and his gifted, gracious wife, Vivian—his companion in every life-enterprise ever set before them. The writer's focus and foremost subject is his wife, and while part of this book's beauty is in how it reflects the dynamism and love that so observably bound their two souls together, Richard writes with more than tender sentiment. Far more, he discloses a power and spiritual discernment as he describes the journey he and Vivian took together. As you read about the heroic qualities of her faith, between the lines you'll inescapably encounter heart-stirring evidences of his own as well. I remember how awesomely moving this was to witness at the time, and I delight to see it chronicled here so warmly and accessibly.

My wife, Anna, and I were honored to be welcomed by Richard and Vivian into their struggle from the beginning. However, we were but a tiny, virtually insignificant fraction of those who watched the unfolding of that kind of miracle that only hope can produce. Since we had navigated Anna's cancer years before, we had faced that beast and under God's mercy received the temporal blessing of a full recovery. But walking with and watching Richard and Vivian, along with their family, friends, and the whole community of the university faculty and student body, we all witnessed something of a more ultimate joy. It was found then, and you can find it here, in the pragmatic vitality that flows toward any of us when we enter that dimension of hope that issues in "dying graces."

It's a hope not rooted in philosophy or even theology—it's found at the fountainhead of relationships. It begins with that relationship gained when we let God's great heart of love embrace us, and it advances as human hearts truly open to what he can do to enable the magnificently heroic even in the middle of the horrendously hellish. Richard and Vivian proved that the power of hope is greater than the power of cancer—as surely as the love of God is greater than life or death, or principalities or powers, or things present or things to come, or height or depth, or any other created thing. (See Romans 8:38-39.)

This hope, born of love's overcoming power, brought victory to the Felixes—a victory gained through the tenacity of their mutually sustaining partnership as they passed into the fiery crucible of cancer. To read their story is to discover the truly miraculous: not in a triumph over disease, but of an awesome, overcoming grace through it. It's the grandest triumph, because it is, indeed, the ultimate one.

—Jack W. Hayford

ACKNOWLEDGMENTS

The School of Dying Graces evolved from a dream I had at Salt Creek Beach a few weeks following Vivian's homegoing. God's promise in the dream was that Vivian would one day see her children and grandchildren in heaven because of her faithfulness to Him.

Soon I came to realize that would only happen if Vivian's remarkable journey was documented and recorded. I was the one person who had been with her 24/7 for nearly thirty months during the struggle with cancer. I had access to all of her journals during that period. God's divine thumb was firmly in my back to let go of the Azusa Pacific presidency and tell her story—not only for her children and grandchildren, but also for the thousands who need hope, a hope that can only be found upon entering into the school of dying graces.

I gratefully offer acknowledgments to my friends at Azusa Pacific University:

The board of trustees who placed great trust in Richard and Vivian in bringing us to APU; gave unwavering, above and beyond support during the darkest hours of our journey; and whose continued prayers and support made this book possible.

To the faculty and staff whose everyday, in-and-out performance resulted in making APU a "flagship university" as acknowledged by the February 2, 2004, issue of *Time* magazine. These women and men exemplify the four cornerstones of APU: Christ, Scholarship, Service, and Community. Their prayers and many acts of kindness will never be forgotten.

To the thousands of students who attended APU during the 1990s. They were the energy of the university. It was their passion to place "God First" that compelled us to accept the presidency at APU. They prayed and fasted around the clock, held prayer vigils outside and around our home, and actually came to the house and laid hands on Vivian, begging God for a miracle. My family and I will never forget their love and passion for our beloved Vivian. This book is their marching manual to practice these dying graces and make them their living graces.

Finally, some personal acknowledgments:

To Vivian's personal assistant, Laura Palusso. At the onset of Vivian's illness the board of trustees approved Laura to assist Vivian full time regardless of the situation and need. Laura was there at the very end. No one should be expected to give so much, but she did. Only God knows the fullness of her gift to Vivian.

To my administrative assistant, Marilyn Schulz, whose friendship with Vivian was unique and special. Through her efforts, my office was able to function efficiently during my many absences during those last months. She sensitively communicated the journey to APU's many constituencies.

To Vivian's sister, Millie Braselton, a godly woman devoted to her family and church. She and Vivian shared a special love during those last months, a love that has impacted our families forever.

To Vivian's niece Shelly Cui, who came from China to stay with us in Wichita in the early 1980s. Vivian helped her complete language studies as well as her bachelor's and master's degrees. During the early stages of Vivian's illness, Shelly asked us to assemble a group of friends to pray with her so she could give her heart and life to Jesus. She is one of Vivian's treasures in heaven.

Vivian and I served twenty-one years in the presidency of two wonderful Christian universities: Friends University in Wichita, Kansas, and Azusa Pacific University in Azusa, California. I wish I could mention each of our friends who contributed so very much to our success at each institution. Of course, I am deeply indebted to the efforts of my agent, Kathy Helmers, and my friend Rob Wilkins for their literary contributions.

Finally, to Vivian's many, many personal friends from college days through our years in Indiana, Tennessee, Florida, Kansas, and California. Many of you have told me that Vivian was your very best friend. I wish that space would allow me to list each and every one of your names.

GRACE FOR
LIVING

1 BRINGER
OF HOPE

Give me a new name, Lord: "Bringer of Hope."
Let me through my experience bring new and
living hope to those who have no hope. Lord God,
I prayed two years ago, "Change me," and you have.
Now let me help others to live the abundant
life in you.

My wife wrote these words from her personal Gethsemane, a place of great suffering that became holy ground for her most intimate encounters with God. I could not follow her there, though I longed to do so with every cell in my body.

I write these words from my own Gethsemane—a garden bereft of her presence, where I have anguished with God and against God. It has become for me the holy ground on which I have tried to retrace her steps along a journey that led her figuratively and literally to the heart of God.

I could not enter with my wife into her school of dying graces. She cannot accompany me now as I harvest these graces for living.

✦ ✦ ✦

Vivian died after an epic struggle with cancer. I had been certain that God would heal her, but God did not answer my prayers for her physical recovery—nor those of my family, our beloved friends, and a vast Christian community who loved us and supported us.

4

One early morning on a very warm day in Southern California, a year and a half after my wife's death, I attended a funeral for the mother of one of my friends. As I was leaving the cemetery, baking in the heat of my car, I pulled off to the side and stepped out of the car to shed my jacket. I folded it carefully and placed it on the backseat. As I shut the back door and turned around to get into the front seat, I found myself looking at a man about fifteen feet away.

He was kneeling at his wife's grave—weeping, calling out her name, telling her how much he missed her. As he fiddled with the flowers in front of him, he occasionally wiped the tears away from his face with the backs of his hands. Then he wailed some more. I stood there like a deer frozen in car headlights. The man suddenly turned and stared at me, and I saw my own face reflected in his. Pain and anguish cut to the core of my heart as I fell into my car and started the engine. But after driving a hundred feet or so, I stopped and crumpled over the steering wheel for several minutes. Grief came roaring into the front room of my very being, routing me from every room of my soul.

I later wrote to a friend:

> *I know that God is working at a deep place in my life. I am*
> *trying to understand each and every thing that is happening to*
> *me. I still journal daily. I will not be the same person at the*
> *end of this journey. Life in the future will be more about being*
> *than it will be about doing. Someday when Vivian and I ren-*
> *dezvous with Jesus, I am sure I will give God thanks for this*
> *season of my life. From a human viewpoint I cannot compre-*
> *hend that truth, but through faith it will be so.*

In the war against my wife's cancer, I had been given a job to
do, eventually assigned to me by Vivian herself: to pray for her
healing, while she prepared herself for dying. During the thirty
months between the day she was diagnosed with breast cancer
and the day she took her last breath on this earth, I abandoned
myself to the task of fervent prayer. Until her dying breath—and,
strangely, for many weeks after— I believed God would intervene
with a miracle of healing for my wife. The more the miracle
seemed delayed, the greater I imagined God's glory when the doctors, with puzzled smiles on their faces, would report that Vivian
was free of cancer.

Inexplicably, nearly two months after my wife's death, I was still
praying for her healing. To this day, it is something I occasionally
catch myself doing. I once read that after the invention of the po-
lio vaccine, fund-raising to battle the disease continued even
though the threat had been eradicated. Once set in motion, with
so much at stake, the charity machine took some time to shut
down. Likewise, I had been fighting the Beast for so long that it
was difficult to relinquish the struggle.

Our thirty-fifth wedding anniversary came in August, following Vivian's death in June. I believed I had failed at my task. Had my faith been greater, had I prayed more consistently and with greater fervor, then Vivian and I would have been celebrating our anniversary together, planning for our next year of ministry at the helm of Azusa Pacific University and future retirement. At that time, my only option besides blaming myself was to blame God.

Since then, on my better days, I have come to see glimpses of God's deeper and mysterious plan. But on that brilliant blue day, my sky was dark. That August afternoon I received a card with a photo of a woman's hand on top of a man's hand. Inside were the words:

God made our hands fit for each other.

Lower, in her own handwriting, my beloved wife had added:

Until our hands will meet together.

Before her death, Vivian had given the card to a friend, who promised to mail it the day before our anniversary. That was like her. She loved gardening, and she understood that a good harvest required loving consistency. I looked out over the garden that she and I had planted and tended together that spring, now overtaken by weeds. I remembered the love Vivian had for the process of growing living fruit: the nurture, the pruning, and the daily care.

With our thirty-fifth anniversary card lying on a nightstand by our bed, I fell asleep, and a terrible, recurring image returned: Vivian's discarded gardening tools, lying on top of the dirt in a careful line—spade, gloves, sunglasses, knee pads, and watering can. I awoke cold with sweat, startled anew: *Vivian is gone.*

As part of my grieving, I read and reread a series of journals that

Vivian kept during her illness. Over and over, through my tears, I was struck with the spiritual passion that had been seeded in her suffering. In reading her journals, I felt as if I were watching it take root, grow, and blossom into an otherworldly beauty. I began taking notes. In an effort to duplicate Vivian's spiritual growth in my own life, I simply retraced her steps—read the books she read, prayed the prayers she did, and followed the spiritual disciplines she had developed.

I had a double purpose in mind: to write a book detailing her experiences, using excerpts from her spiritual journal, and to heal my own heart. In the summer of that same year, I spent nearly every day in the library—reading the desert fathers and mothers, taking notes on prayer techniques, exploring solitude and silence, and imprinting the Word on my heart.

For a long time, for whatever reason, neither the healing nor the book came to me. Despite my best efforts to seek God, I felt incapacitated by an unmoving despair. A good deal more time passed before any light interrupted the darkness that surrounded me. Like rays bent into the colors of a rainbow after a terrible storm, my periods of healing have come slowly, unexpectedly, as pure gifts of God's grace.

✦ ✦ ✦

In the days leading up to her death, Vivian had been wearing a necklace I gave her on our thirty-third wedding anniversary. It had been specially made as a heart in two pieces—one half for her to wear, the other for me, symbolizing the never-ending wholeness of our love. After she passed away, we realized that Vivian's necklace had mysteriously disappeared. In the coming months, I found my-self searching desperately for the necklace. Over and over, I pleaded with God for the grace to find the jewelry.

On the first anniversary of her death, I was exploring one of the closets in our old home, trying to find a place to store some boxes of baseball cards. As I stepped behind one of the boxes, I noticed a small dancing light from the corner of my eye. I looked down to discover Vivian's necklace, its pendant cut to the shape of an R. In haste, I reached for the necklace around my own neck—its pendant cut to the shape of a V—and put the two halves together. Once again, it fit to form one heart.

Now, four years after my wife's death, I have begun to understand how my own broken heart can begin to mend as I live a new season of life without her. I can see the impact of Vivian's life and death in the faith and lives of hundreds—perhaps thousands—of people. In the way she faced adversity with faith and died with grace, she planted seeds that were already ripening into a great harvest.

Two of Vivian's favorite verses were John 12:24 and Romans 8:28.

> I tell you the truth, unless a kernel of wheat falls to
> the ground and dies, it remains only a single seed.
> But if it dies, it produces many seeds.

> And we know that in all things God works for the
> good of those who love him, who have been called
> according to his purpose.

Through the eyes of faith, Vivian came to grips with the paradox that in the process of our suffering and dying, God's greater purpose

8

of life in full can be revealed. Through obedience unto death, Vivian began to catch glimpses of God working through her to accomplish purposes far greater than her own physical healing. More and more, she understood her faith was influencing others and weaving threads of God's present redemption into his eternal plan:

> *I don't know why I am dying of cancer when you could have healed me at any point during treatment, but I know I can live for you today. Lord, make me beautiful of soul, and then let others see into my soul. Let my mind constantly be on you. Let me play the game of minutes and utilize my time to pray for others. Expand my life outward, Lord. Let my life have ultimate meaning. Allow me to bring hope and your love to others.*

9

Vivian lived longer—and better—than anyone could have imagined. Second Corinthians 4:16–5:1 paints the picture:

> Therefore we do not lose heart. Though outwardly we are wasting away, yet inwardly we are being renewed day by day. For our light and momentary troubles are achieving for us an eternal glory that far outweighs them all. So we fix our eyes not on what is seen, but on what is unseen. For what is seen is temporary, but what is unseen is eternal. Now we know that if the earthly tent we live in is destroyed, we have a building from God, an eternal house in heaven, not built by human hands.

Beyond the inevitable, devouring, and pain-filled path of a terrible enemy, in circular lines of communion, my wife increasingly entered into the presence of the Eternal One. Through private prayer, immersion in the Word, obedience, and heartfelt worship, she was able to learn eternal lessons of God's power and goodness.

> *Lord Jesus, I have prayed again and again for you to give me new eyes to see you ever present. And you have. You have allowed me to see beyond the visible to the Kingdom that connects and overlaps with our present world. I have seen you in power and might. I pray your presence would be so real to me that I might live and rejoice as one transformed into your image.*

10

My wife became a bringer of hope to thousands of people—hope that suffering can teach us how to live well, hope that while evil can ravage the body it cannot conquer the soul, hope that God will come to us in the very place where we are certain we have been abandoned.

Could my wife, after her death, become a bringer of hope to me? The question tortured me during the most intense phases of my grieving. I had been dealt the blow of losing all my hopes. My heart waited by the gate for her return, intent only on the sight of her coming back to me, while I tried to move mind and body forward without her.

This story is, in a sense, my answer to that question. Yes, it is possible to find hope beyond the death of all earthly hopes. It is possible to stand on the cusp of our very worst fears, endure the nightmare of their coming true, and find that on the other side we have been transformed rather than destroyed.

My turning point came as I gave myself to the graces of living that were forged in my wife's victorious dying:

- *The grace of letting go*—to hold with open hands what we are most afraid of losing, and to cling only to what we cannot lose.
- *The grace of seeing with the eyes of faith*—to be willing to see the greater miracles God may have for us.
- *The grace of dependence*—to give up control and embrace brokenness as a path to greater intimacy with God.
- *The grace of surrender*—to embrace suffering as a friend rather than fearing it as an enemy.
- *The grace of gratitude*—to be thankful for the beauty at the heart of life, even in the horror and disfigurement of disease.
- *The grace of transformation*—to cling to the transforming power of God's love.

In death and in life, I am learning, we are offered grace upon grace. The lessons may be costly, but the wisdom is priceless.

THE GRACE
OF LETTING GO

2

TO HOLD LIGHTLY
THE THINGS
OF THIS WORLD

On November 20, 1998, in a windowless room
of grays and antiseptic steel, Vivian's oncologist
took off her white coat, hung it on the back of
the door, and climbed up on the examining table
with my wife. She put her arm around Vivian.
There was, she began, no easy way to put this
into words: The Beast would win.

The Beast is what Vivian had named her breast
cancer—a rare and voracious form diagnosed less
than two years earlier, seeded in a 2.5-centimeter
tumor on the lower left quadrant of her left breast.
Dr. Lucille Leong, a brilliant and kind woman
who like my wife had a Chinese heritage, had become a friend. At the City of Hope, a cancer center and research institute near Los Angeles, the

final prognosis was wrapped in a hug. Although the news came as a terrible blow, like having the air knocked out of you on a subzero day, it did not come as a surprise.

The Beast was an accurate name for her disease. The inflammatory breast cancer stalked and ravaged my beautiful wife. Into its path we threw the best medical artillery—a lumpectomy, three rounds of chemotherapy, a double mastectomy, radiation of the lungs and brain, a bone marrow transplant, a miracle drug, and experimental therapies. Vivian left behind a medical chronology that, single-spaced, covered more than eight pages. From February 1997 until that smoggy Southern California afternoon when our medical options came to an end, the Beast never wavered a single step. The prayers for healing—thousands, tens of thousands of them—also failed to break its terrifying track.

In a room designed for efficiency, the doctor's words ringing in our ears, I cupped Vivian's face in my hands. As her eyes filled with tears, she reached her hands to mine. I have always relished my wife's touch, the softest and most wonderful feeling in the world. Even with the prognosis, I could not force myself to believe that her life—and by a different measure, mine—would soon be over.

We had believed Vivian would be healed. By the grace of God, the wonder of technology, or an impressive combination, we were certain she would live to see each of her children's children. There was always reason for hope.

Shortly before her cancer diagnosis, Vivian even received what she thought was an image of healing. She wrote in her journal:

As I was praying I visualized my heart and on the left lower side there was a wound. As I watched it, the wound festered and came to a head. A tumor came out of it, fell, and was planted in the soil. After a while, a plant grew up and blossomed. I was left with the picture of a single green plant with a single stalk and, at the top, a lovely heart-shaped flower.

As we left the City of Hope after hundreds of visits, we made it a custom to point out the sign near the water fountain:

> *There Is Always Hope*

Even when told our medical options were exhausted, we were fully prepared for the bloom of miracle.

"You can expect four to six weeks," Dr. Leong had said. After hearing the doctor's words, Vivian climbed down from the examining table and asked me to take her to the beach. This was not a surprise. The beach was her place of refuge and renewal. Shortly after moving from Kansas to California in 1990, when I assumed the position of president of Azusa Pacific University, we bought a condominium overlooking Dana Point, an hour's drive south of Los Angeles. Over the years, the beach became our cherished spot. After long hours of working together toward lofty goals of higher Christian education, we would come and sit, side by side, listening to the pounding surf and watching the sunset. The beach always made us think of God—his power, grace, and majesty.

At times we desperately needed to be reminded of his presence. The evening following Vivian's doctor's prognosis, we knew, would be one of those times. Aware that we would need some time away following the doctor's appointment, we had packed our bags for the weekend. After receiving her prognosis, I wheeled Vivian down the halls and out next to the fountain by the City of Hope. I pulled our black SUV around and gently placed her in the seat on the passenger side, the chair fully tilted back. She closed her eyes. As we silently drove away, it was the first time we failed to point out the sign reminding us of hope.

Moving toward the foothills of the San Gabriel Mountains, I looked over at my wife and thought of a few prayers in the always-moving river of pleas to God on her behalf. *Dear Lord, my job has been to pray nonstop, day and night, for a miracle. Every day for two years, thousands of prayers have been said for my Vivian; hundreds of students have prayed and fasted around the clock. Where are you?* It hit me then with a terrible ringing of unexpected surprise: My wife, barring a last-minute miracle, would die at the age of fifty-five. On our thirty-fifth wedding anniversary, I would be left alone to figure out where to go.

When I turned onto I-210, heading for 605 South, I felt my wife's soft hand gently squeezing my forearm. I looked over, and though her eyes were still closed, I could see tears pooling, beginning to fall. My hands scrambled for Kleenex, and finding none, I looked over again. She was wearing a smile, white and frail like a crescent moon. With her expression, she told me I didn't need to worry.

For the next few minutes, we rode in silence, both of us lost in our own thoughts. When I saw motion in my peripheral vision, I looked over at Vivian. She was gently moving her arm in a circular fashion and at first I did not understand. When she motioned again—toward the driver's side—I looked at my speedometer. I was

moving at forty-five miles per hour, the speed on California free-
ways at which some people, as the joke goes, change a tire. I do not
have a reputation for moving so slowly; in fact, some of the students
had nicknamed me Parnelli, after the legendary auto racer of the
1960s. Obediently I moved over a lane and accelerated. A few moments later, Vivian motioned again. I moved over another lane and
sped up. A few moments later, she motioned again. I moved another
lane over and sped up. A few moments later, I looked over and she
was moving her lips, but I could not decipher what she was saying.

"Car-pool lane," she finally said distinctly.

She wanted me to cross over—illegally—into the far left lane. I
smiled at my wife's first words since we left the City of Hope.
When her mind was set on a thing, she could be like that: strong
willed and—mostly without her awareness—controlling. Who
could blame her? She did not want to miss the sunset on the beach.
We both pictured the place she had in mind. After world explorer
and writer Richard Henry Dana discovered the point in 1835, he
called it "the only romantic spot in California"—a natural sand
beach, nestled in a cove between two green knolls, towering cliffs,
and the tide-pulled waves of the Pacific Ocean. As Vivian fell
asleep, I knew she was dreaming of that spot—the low evening
slant of light, the deep blues and hazy scarlet, the sound of lovers
posing for pictures at sunset.

✦ ✦ ✦

Following a beautiful sunset at the beach, we ate at the Harbor
Grill, a restaurant overlooking a thousand ships. Vivian, as was her
custom, ordered lamb. I chose the gumbo lobster soup, New

Orleans style. We had walked slowly, arm in arm, down the hill from our condominium, processing what was impossible to understand. *Four to six weeks.* There was much that needed to be said. We sat at a candlelit outdoor table on the veranda. We talked but with few words. I wanted her to take the lead, to release her thoughts, but she deserved to move at her own pace. We spoke of our three grown children.

"Do you think Doak likes his new job?" she asked with some concern.

"He seems excited about it," I replied.

20

"Do you remember the lake condo we rented in the Rockies with Melissa and Lance?" I asked.

"Oh, the moon reflecting on the water was so beautiful," she said.

"Tris is working on his first big case," she said. "I think he's going to move up quickly in the firm, don't you?"

"His personality and spirit suit him well," I replied.

"We need to call them about the news," Vivian said.

"We'll do that tomorrow," I replied.

Then, a silence enveloped us. Not knowing where to focus tearing eyes, Vivian looked down at my chest and then, a few moments later, up at my hairline. I rolled my eyes in the same directions—up or down—trying to follow her thoughts. She smiled. We were at our getaway, our table, overlooking the harbor. When the waiter inquired about dessert, I joked with her: "I guess I'll order one, since you never do."

She knew the punch line: "So I can eat it." I ordered something outrageous, a chocolate raspberry mousse, I think. As we waited, I caught her looking at me in a way I had not noticed before. She was studying my face. I tried to calculate what it was she was seeing.

What? I asked with my eyes.

Vivian's tears came. When she looked down, I cupped her chin, raising her head gently. I still remember the look of terrible disappointment and hurt: *This is not what we had planned.* From this same restaurant, watching the ships sail in and out, we had talked of our rapidly approaching years of retirement: of the rest and joy we might find; of repeating the names, one by one, of our grandchildren; of the sunsets we would watch, side by side. We had planned on many full years, not a few short weeks.

Vivian could not stop crying. I got up and wrapped her in a shawl. When she leaned into me, I could feel her weakness. Uncharacteristically she lost control. As the waiter awkwardly arrived with our dessert, I told Vivian it didn't matter who was watching. Whenever she was ready, I would put my hand in hers, and at whatever pace she chose, we would walk together up the hill, back through pastel colors of night to the place we had come to love.

21

✦ ✦ ✦

In our place by the ocean, Vivian fell asleep listening to the rhythm of waves through open windows. She was too exhausted to participate in our necessary nightly procedures of cleansing and bandaging. Across my wife's chest—ravaged by surgery, radiation, and ghastly experiments—I gently applied salve and looked into her sleeping and peaceful face. "Thank you, Richard," she usually told me before falling asleep, "for loving me *like this.*"

My wife, before her cancer, had such beautiful breasts, full and curving.

The routine was the same: Remove fluids, put on various salves and ointments, and cover her with bandages, which formed an artificial and protective layer of skin. As I worked my hands across her chest, I couldn't help but feel some relief: Her suffering would be over soon. Such peace would be permanent. I remembered what Vivian told me once at the beach near twilight. Pointing out the white silver of the water's foaming edge—the way it seemed unexpectedly bright—she smiled and guessed it might be a color one could expect to see in heaven.

Alongside the tenderness, anger rose inside of me. She had fought such a good fight against such an unrelenting and merciless foe. Never once did she blame God. Cleaning the places where my wife's breasts once were, touching those tender and ravaged places, all I could feel was the injustice. Just what did it take to prompt a good and gracious God to heal one of his beloved?

I had wanted so badly to know; I could do so little for her.

With the doctor's hopeless prognosis running through my head, I lost myself in the grace of a practiced and loving ritual. My hands moved to the rhythm of the crashing surf outside our bedroom window. The balm was supposed to heal.

◆ ◆ ◆

The next morning, sitting beside my wife in a cove discovered by a fearless explorer, I realized that one of the reasons my wife loved the beach was that it provided a necessary perspective. In an artist's curve of line, the distance was always a fluid uncertainty, and beyond that lay an end you simply had to take by faith. With limited sight, a certain courage was required to explore the places that appeared to form the sharp edge of a fading earth. On that morning Vivian could see with the eyes of faith. Like a slowly developing Polaroid, the outlines were still fuzzy, but the impression for her was finally clear.

Vivian told me she needed to prepare to die. Following a string of terrible losses, she was letting go of her final possession: her life. She asked me for a favor. Torn between praying for healing and for the grace to die, she no longer possessed the energy to balance such a volatile paradox. She wanted to know if I would take over her prayers for a miracle. I told her I had always faithfully prayed for healing and would be glad to assume the further responsibility to pray on her behalf.

Even before the doctor confirmed our worst fears, Vivian knew she would not be healed—physically, at least. After a biopsy revealed a new tumor, following a grueling bone marrow transplant, Vivian wrote in a journal entry dated September 19, 1998:

> I started this [journal] to record my journey to wellness.
> I have not done well by it. But today I am impressed to
> change it to a record of my spiritual journey. For 21 months I
> have prayed for healing. I have begged God, badgered, pleaded,
> wept, screamed, yelled at, tried to manipulate, shamed,
> reminded—every tactic I could think of—and I have
> expressed every emotion felt by one who is dying of cancer.
> I have prayed for a sign, asked and hoped for a sign that the
> Lord would heal me. Nothing has come.
>
> All I seem to get is, "Trust me."
>
> Lord, you have heard hundreds and thousands of prayers for
> me. I have accused you of sitting on your throne with your
> arms folded, disregarding those pleas. Forgive me—you

know my human flesh and struggles with roller-coaster emotions. Sometimes I would like even just a few days of release from the fear and knowledge of cancer.

But I know in my heart that you are good and loving and the giver of peace. So now I ask that you turn my mind and my heart from my illness to you. I am ready. "Nothing in my hand I bring, only to the cross I cling."

On the beach as Vivian held my hand, she returned me to a snapshot from our past—a few years before our move to California. After reading Hannah Whitall Smith's *The Christian's Secret to a Happy Life*, she had made two simple requests: to praise God in everything and to hold lightly the things of this world. She was beginning to realize how those prayers, accelerated since her cancer diagnosis and often camouflaged by overwhelming suffering, had been answered by God.

For whatever short time might remain, she said she needed to turn her focus away from the disease and onto the presence of God. She told me she planned to enroll in the school of dying graces. Certainly Vivian had matriculated at the undergraduate level. Now she would move on to graduate studies where she would major in suffering and learn new languages of disappointment and joy. As she turned to ask me if I understood, I marveled at her faith. In her battles with the Beast, Vivian had encountered enormous losses: her health, appearance, breasts, dignity, certainty, and need for a measure of control. In a literal fashion, piece by piece by piece, she was losing little bits of her self. In her journal, she once recorded:

It is so hard to die in slow pieces. It is so hard to suffer.

"But, Vivian, God will heal you," I told her that morning, as I had so many times before. She smiled, and I knew with a sudden, piercing pang: She was letting go of me also.

A few days before Vivian's death, we set up a hospice in our living room. Just before she slipped into a coma and required oxygen to breathe, I positioned her bed for the best view out the French doors overlooking the back patio and garden. On a bright Mother's Day five years earlier, I had planted Vivian a rosebush. In clear sight of her bed, the rosebush was now in full bloom. Rising on a single stalk, high above a mass of stunning white blossoms, was a greening stem. At the top was a lovely crimson heart-shaped flower.

25

3 WHEN FEAR FIRST HITS

Vivian discovered the lump on her left breast during the fall of 1996. In the pages of her first cancer journal, she wrote of that moment.

When I first found the lump, I was unbelieving. I decided it had to be just some hard tissue—it was so large I was sure it could not be a tumor. I put it out of my mind and checked it in a few weeks—still there. Then Melissa was coming to plan her wedding. And Christmas was no time to go to the doctor. Then came the board meetings and the Florida trip. I knew we had to see a doctor when we returned. Spending a whole night up with cystitis again told me some things can't be put off.

Vivian did not tell me about the doctor's appointment she scheduled for January 28, 1997. When the receptionist had asked for the reason for her visit, Vivian said she was having hot flashes. She could be at the onset of menopause. She would mention the lump to the doctor later, as an aside. On the surface, Vivian had not panicked. She had had lumps before, and they proved to be benign false alarms.

> *It never occurred to me I might have breast cancer—*
> *no family history, no bad habits such as being overweight,*
> *no smoking, no alcohol.*

When the doctor found the lump on her breast, he was no longer concerned about Vivian's menopause.

> *I could see the alarm on his face when he felt the lump.*
> *After that he was very quiet. He could tell it was not a cyst.*
> *He said he wanted me to see an oncologist immediately—*
> *he would call and set the appointment. He also said he*
> *wanted me to go immediately to the lab and radiology and*
> *get a sonogram and a mammogram.*

The tests took hours. At our home, I received a call from Vivian's secretary saying she might be late for our dinner with friends, who were visiting us from out of state. She had been unexpectedly delayed at the doctor's office. I wondered: *The doctor's office?*

From our living room, I saw my wife pull in the driveway and then back up and park on the street. I thought that was unusual but kept talking with our friends. When she stayed in the car for a while, I suspected she might be listening to a radio program. When she bent her head over the steering wheel, I believed she might be praying. I excused myself to check on her.

I was hoping when I drove home that our friends and Richard had already gone to dinner so I could go into my room and cry, but they were all there in the living room talking. Richard came out to the car.

"I heard you went to the doctor—why didn't you tell me?"

Vivian started to cry.

"The doctor found a lump on my breast," Vivian told me. "He thinks it's cancer."

I wrapped her in my arms. I did not understand it then, but I do now: That was the last normal day of our lives. Vivian put her arm around my shoulder and we walked to our bedroom. I returned to tell our guests she was not feeling well. I told them I thought it would be best if we let her rest and went to dinner without her.

The next day and a half passed in a fog. Richard was sure it would be a benign lump. But in my deepest heart I knew— and knew from the beginning—that it was cancer, although it took me a long time to admit it.

Vivian and I met with a doctor on our HMO plan at 11 AM on Thursday—two days after her first visit. It was his responsibility to tell us if our lives were about to change forever. In a small examining room of grays and silvers under cold fluorescent light, he never extended his hand in greeting. Instead, he walked up to my wife and examined the lump. When he finished, he told Vivian to get dressed and meet him in his office.

29

Richard and I went into his office and sat down. He came in and barely sat down before he said, "You have a malignant tumor and it has to come out right away. I recommend a radical mastectomy."

I was still waiting for hello.

At this point, the nurse/receptionist, who cracked her gum a good deal, interrupted with a question. The tears started down Vivian's face; I held her, trying myself not to grimace in response to the blows of such brutal and uncaring words.

Richard took my hand. The doctor said, "Sorry to sledgehammer you, but there really is no easy way to break the news."

He suggested we go ahead and schedule the surgery for the next Monday.

The phone rang and, incredibly, the doctor accepted the call.

He also recommended I have the ovaries removed at the same time—not saying, but indicating, that it might also be ovarian cancer.

The nurse/receptionist interrupted with another message.

He then gave me a booklet on mastectomies published by the state.

Again the phone rang and the doctor talked to someone else. He didn't even apologize for the interruption.

He said, "When you get out of the hospital, they will ask you if you have read it. I don't care if you do or don't, but if you don't, lie and say you did."

The nurse/receptionist entered again.

He gave me a list of things to do before Monday and then rose and left the office. I was numb. I went home and cried and tried to pull myself together.

As was her nature, Vivian did not stay down long. She had to call and ask her coworkers for help: Lynnette would need to take over several projects, Roxane would have to cancel her participation in the ministry conference, and she needed Laura to help her find our son Doak, who was living at home. Vivian also wanted to fix lunch for those who dropped by to see how they might help. In a busy attention to details, she tried to distract herself from the buzz of such words as *cancer* and *surgery on Monday*. Perfunctorily, the doctor had told us not to wait. He had added "radical" to mastectomy. As he kept referring to my wife's breasts as "both of those things," he stressed urgency. We needed time to think, the very thing the doctor said we did not possess.

It so happened that we had previously set a date on our calendar for a dinner that evening with Jack and Anna Hayford. I called Jack—pastor of the Church on the Way and a casual friend—and told him of our bad news. Jack and Anna were gracious enough to drive to a restaurant in our area for dinner.

We went to Femino's and had a nice time. It turned out that Anna had colon cancer several years ago and they knew the fear that comes with cancer. After eating, we went to our house and prayed. Jack had Richard stand behind me and put his hands on my shoulder while Anna put her hand on my chest. It was a powerful time.

The Hayfords offered no miracles for healing or certainties of deliverance. They offered just two suggestions, which would later prove to be lifelines:

♦ Don't be afraid to be afraid.
♦ Let others serve you.

THE GRACE
OF SEEING WITH
THE EYES OF FAITH

4 PRAYING FOR A MIRACLE

In Vivian's mind, a coincidence was no accident. In her journal, she quoted Bernie Siegel: "A coincidence is God's way of remaining anonymous." Unbeknownst to us, on the day of Vivian's brutal diagnosis, a faculty member at the Azusa Pacific University nursing school and one of Vivian's good friends placed a call to the vice president of nursing at the City of Hope. The VP, an APU nursing graduate, immediately set up an appointment for Vivian with Dr. Lawrence Wagman, the chief surgeon at the City of Hope.

At 11 AM on Friday, Vivian met with Dr. Wagman.

He did a very thorough exam—both breasts, lymph nodes, abdomen. He took my

35

case history personally. In all, he spent two hours with us—amazing. He carefully explained everything—all options and all ramifications. He then did a fine-needle biopsy, which we did not know was even a possibility. He also scheduled the pre-op tests for Wednesday and the surgery for Thursday. After the exam, he very carefully eased us into the possibility it might be cancer. He said the biopsy would tell us definitely.

After our meeting with Dr. Wagman, Vivian and I felt renewed confidence. We focused on this new direction, which Dr. Wagman had presented with such compassion.

✦ ✦ ✦

Every crisis happens in a context of community. After her initial diagnosis, Vivian and I never hesitated about sharing her journey with the campus body of Azusa Pacific University. We believed in the power of prayer when shared by a fellowship. In many ways, as one of my staff said later, it was like having the back of your hospital gown open. We downplayed whatever risks or embarrassment; Vivian and I knew we needed community, the local outworking of the body of Christ. We would have not survived any other way.

On the morning of January 31, 1997, while Vivian and I were at the City of Hope to hear her biopsy results, the APU chapel was charged to pray for Vivian. As a community, sharing the body of Christ, we lifted our requests for God's mercy. Could a miracle be out of the question? Since our arrival in 1990, we had become convinced of God's direct intervention on behalf of a praying community. On campus, God accomplished many things far beyond our individual or collective power. Our size and enrollment had nearly doubled, but more importantly the university was in the process of recapturing some of its most powerful beliefs: Prayer matters. Faith works. God can be trusted. As early as 1993—four years before my wife's diagnosis—we felt a rooting in one of the university's fundamental beliefs. In a campus magazine, I had written:

> Those of you who have had a long acquaintance with APU know that for 31 years Dr. Cornelius Haggard believed and repeated this phrase over and over, "Expect a miracle." I believe indeed this has become an attitudinal mind-set for the institution and provided a deep assurance that surely God's hand is on the university. And with the multitude of accompanying prayers, the miracles at APU have never ceased.

37

Early on in my presidency at APU, I worked hard at restoring the correct order of things: God first. In the four corners of the school's new logo were: Christ, Community, Service, and Scholarship. Through cycles of brokenness and healing, Vivian and I had worked—and prayed—for spiritual renewal. On campus, there was a feeling that anything might happen.

While Vivian and I were at the hospital getting the news from Dr. Wagman that she did indeed have cancer, thousands of prayers were lifted in the bond of shared belief for Vivian's healing. Despite the dark news, we felt light because we knew God was a God of hope and healing. Who could doubt it? Expect a miracle.

Richard and I felt like a great dark cloud had lifted. We went to the Crocodile Café for lunch. Jon Wallace [APU vice president] delivered the box of comments from chapel each of the students had written. It was truly uplifting.

When we left the café, renewed in hope and faith, I remember it being a warm day. We felt a cool salt breeze slide over a blue ocean. With boxes full of prayers, a City of Hope in our own backyard, and God undeniably for us, Vivian and I were beginning to believe this would be a fight that, however terrible, we could not lose.

As we held on to each other's hands, we shared a certain hope.

38

5 TO LIVE
A FULL LIFE

When I called with news of her mother's cancer, I was unaware of our daughter Melissa's recent fears that something terrible was about to strike our family. Months after her mother's death she finally told me of her dark premonitions, which would sometimes double her over with a sick feeling.

Normally optimistic people like Melissa are not good at handling sinking dread. From the beginning, she says now, she understood her mother was going to die.

Out of her office when I had phoned, Melissa casually returned my call. It was no surprise she could only pick out—and connect together—two of my words: *mother* and *cancer*.

Her fiancé, Lance, had to drive her home from the office. She says it was the closest she has ever come to hysteria. In an odd fashion, her dark premonitions served her well: She had, in critical ways, already prepared herself for the worst. With great courage, she picked herself off the bed, packed her bags, and left the next morning for a fourteen-hour drive from her home in Denver to Los Angeles. She told Lance good-bye, perhaps until the wedding. Driving through the plains and deserts and mountains, she fought against a descending and grim reality. As the landscapes blended into one another, she shielded herself with good memories with all of her heart.

She remembered how thrilled her mother had been to hear of her engagement. Vivian, too, had fallen in love with Lance. Shortly after the announcement, Melissa took a week of vacation to be with her mother to plan the wedding. Together they had picked out a dress, a church overlooking the ocean, and a reception hall by the harbor. She remembered how her mother had responded when, sifting through an endless number of beautiful dresses, Melissa had asked her how she could ever choose one. "Just like you did a husband," Vivian said. "You'll just know it's right."

They had eaten at ocean-side tables and discussed themes, backdrops, dates, places, invitations, sunsets, churches, and flowers. Vivian was focused on making Melissa's wedding special.

With two months until her wedding day, bleary-eyed with tears and miles, Melissa pulled into our drive, walked through the front door, jogged down the hall, saw her mother, and ran to hug her. In each other's arms, they cried for a little while. For the longest time in the onslaught of bad news, Melissa held firm.

It wasn't until her mother asked Melissa to sit with her on the bed that the new reality hit. They chatted for a while, and without warning, her mother asked Melissa if she would like to touch the lump. Melissa wanted to say no, but how does one refuse a request like that? As Vivian guided her daughter's hand over her left breast, then adjusted her fingers gently, Melissa felt the cancer—its size and hardness—and wept.

It was at that moment everything changed for my daughter.

✦ ✦ ✦

A week or so after Melissa's arrival, the day before Vivian's lumpectomy, mother and daughter resumed wedding plans. They visited caterers, outlet malls, party stores, and ministers. They laughed a good deal. Vivian wanted her daughter to know that the cancer would not rob either of them of the joy of her wedding. Melissa knew that was true. It just might get mixed up with other things.

In her journal of that day's events, after thanking the Lord for a wonderful time with her daughter, Vivian wrote:

> *I am trying to rejoice and praise you in the midst of my difficulties and fears, but at the same time I don't like it and I want everything to go back to how it used to be— when all was well with my world. Now my world and my future are different. I will live with cancer as a reality for the rest of my life.*

We met again with Dr. Wagman a few days after my wife's lumpectomy. He thoroughly and tenderly examined my wife.

> *He again spent over an hour with us. Dr. Wagman brought in a medical student while he talked to us about the pathology report. He said I have two kinds of*

cancer—noninvasive lobular and ductal—but the larger part of the tumor was metastatic cancer. The tissue above the tumor had no signs of cancer. There were a number of small cysts as well on the tumor. The bad news was that there was cancer in the lymph nodes. This totally changed the prognosis. He said he would send me to the oncologist, who would devise the treatment plan. As he began to talk about hormones and chemotherapy, I began to feel the tears coming down my cheeks.

Dr. Wagman tried to be optimistic and said the good sign was only the lymph nodes closest to the breast were affected. He examined the sutures and said everything looked good. He told us to call Dr. Lucille Leong, the oncologist, to confirm our appointment.

On the weekend after Vivian was discharged from the hospital, missing the first piece of herself, the two of us packed our bags for our condominium at Dana Point. We took an evening walk on the Aliso Creek pier and heard the ocean's roar and the gulls sounding their lonely and laughing calls. We were reminded again of why we loved the sea. This was for us, hand in hand, as close as we would ever get to heaven, which we believed, upon either of our arrivals, would have the feel of sand between our toes and a moon on the horizon.

In the deep purple fall of twilight, neither of us said much. Only occasionally did we interrupt each other's attention to the sound of the ocean. As we walked on the beach, we both understood a fight with cancer, win or lose, changed everything. Our confidence, however, was rooted in deeper realities. With its power to pull and heal, the ocean was one of these. If you have never experienced a campfire at the beach with a night full of stars, I cannot attempt to explain its mysterious beauty and power. There, more than anywhere, we felt close to God. And to each other.

We had invited our three children to join us at the condo so we could talk as a family about Vivian's diagnosis. But Vivian wanted time alone before Melissa, Doak, and Tris arrived, which I was happy to give her. She wanted to figure out what to say to them about her cancer. Standing on the front porch on the morning of February 21, 1997, she welcomed each one of her children to our place by the ocean.

43

We spent the day—from 11 to 3—at Aliso Creek Beach. It was a beautiful day, sunny and 70 degrees with no wind. I took a long walk with Tris and we looked at the tide pools. We got sandwiches at the pier for lunch. When we came back to the apartment, Melissa, Doak, and Richard and I went to the hot tub. After that, we watched Star Wars at Ocean Ranch. It was fun to see it again.

I had told Richard I wanted to sit and talk as a family, so we did. Mostly I talked. I told them about the cancer, the statistics, the treatment. I told them I had been evaluating and rethinking my life. I told them it was an opportunity for me to become the person God meant me to be. And it was a challenge to live life to its fullest. We all talked about shortcomings, difficulties, and grace. I think we all sensed our love for one another. It was a good time and I think a time that will be significant in their lives.

6 CLINGING
TO THE CROSS

On the afternoon following Vivian's first meeting with her oncologist, we were to leave for a weekend getaway at another of our favorite beachside havens, near Santa Barbara, California. We planned to rejoice. We were certain that the thousands of prayers had found their way to a loving God and that Vivian would be better. At Cambria, a secluded beach community nestled in a forest of firs, we would light a fire at twilight, as was our custom, lean against a skull-white log of driftwood, and offer up our praise to God.

With our bags already packed for the trip, we walked across the parking lot at the City of Hope with no small confidence. At some point, we knew we could expect a miracle. Why not now?

Down long halls, up an elevator, we were led into a small waiting room for our first meeting with Dr. Lucille Leong. She shook our hands and smiled. It was a shaky smile.

Dr. Leong handed us copies of Vivian's pathology report. Illustrating on a piece of graph paper, she carefully explained each of the prognostic factors—tests designed to determine a cancer's tenacity and ability to spread. Vivian and I never could have imagined such bad news. On each of the eight factors, Vivian scored on the wrong side. Emerging from dark and vague outlines, as a predator does, Vivian's cancer only slowly revealed itself. This was our first terrifying glimpse—a look over the shoulder at something moving threateningly in the distance.

As Dr. Leong explained each test, she told Vivian to imagine a balancing scale weighing pluses and minuses.

With every cancer, Dr. Leong explained, two factors are critical:

- How fast are its cells dividing?
- Are those cells spreading to other parts of the body?

Even with state-of-the-art technology, medical science cannot fully answer those questions. The best to be hoped for are educated hints—information coupled with intuition. A biopsy provides the raw material—the "fresh specimens," as the report phrased it—for a series of tests, which provide indicators of a cancer's aggressiveness.

As she stared at the minus sign next to each of the first three tests, I could see Vivian was no longer thinking about Cambria, where we had planned to talk about our future once again while the sea lions basked in the sun.

We should not have been so surprised. As the fourth and fifth results were explained, Vivian lost all traces of her smile.

We firmly believed God would heal her. If the prayers of one righteous man were capable of much, what about the prayers of thousands and thousands? The terror of the meeting was in stark contrast to our hope.

We tried to take some comfort in her stage II diagnosis. According to Dr. Leong, more than 70 percent of women in this category survive for at least five years. In a stage III diagnosis that figure drops to less than 50 percent. Vivian's diagnosis was calculated primarily on the basis of her tumor's size—2.5 centimeters. All of the other calculations were not nearly as generous. Vivian's pathology report, unfolding terribly before us, indicated the cancer to be highly aggressive and the body's natural immunity to be severely depressed. Dr. Leong suggested an aggressive treatment plan of several sessions of radiation and chemotherapy.

✦ ✦ ✦

On the way to Cambria, a low fog along the ocean and mountains forced us to exit at Santa Barbara, a small city with homes rising on hills like a dome. We stopped at a hotel for the night. Cambria seemed to both of us a distant dream. Our secret place of escape and refuge was more a distant memory than a present hope. We did not know if we had the necessary energy for the rest of the drive.

> *Santa Barbara was absolutely beautiful and we loved it, but it was difficult to be happy. Most of the time we lay on the bed, hugged each other, and cried.*

I understood Vivian wanted to be alone with God. Heavy with terrible news, I walked the beach at Santa Barbara alone. In solitude, Vivian prayed, read Scriptures, listened to music, and began to contemplate God on a different level. That evening, on three-by-five cards, Vivian and I began to record verses:

> "But I will restore you to health and heal your wounds," declares the Lord.
> (Jeremiah 30:17)

> If you make the Most High your dwelling—
> even the Lord, who is my refuge—
> then no harm will befall you,
> no disaster will come near your tent.
> (Psalm 91:9-10)

> *Therefore, strengthen your feeble arms and weak knees. "Make level paths for your feet," so that the lame may not be disabled, but rather healed.*
> *(Hebrews 12:12-13)*

Between us, we formed a faith pact to pray for her restoration, which would serve the twin purposes of her own maturity through suffering and the giving of glory to God.

> *Give me strength to suffer well. I believe you will heal me.*

As Vivian strained to focus with eyes of faith, all she could make out was the outline of a cross. On such a threatening horizon, what possible good waited to be redeemed?

> *Our life as we have known it is over. But we do have the promise of a new life—more and abundant faith in Christ.*

Early the next morning we got back on the road to Cambria. As we were driving, Vivian suddenly asked me to find a church. Shortly after her request we spotted the highway sign:

> **Mission La
> Purísima Concepción
> EXIT 1 MILE**

Coincidentally, the mission was named for the Immaculate Conception, a holiday celebrated on December 8—also Vivian's birthday. High above La Purísima Concepción, up a winding and shrub-choked hill, I am convinced Vivian saw the cross when we pulled into the parking lot. I did not.

50

We decided to tour the mission, which was originally built in 1787 and had miraculously survived nearly every natural and unnatural disaster imaginable: drought, fire, Indian attack, flood, and hostile takeover, to mention just a few. At one point in its history, we learned, it had been nearly buried under the high desert's sand and silt. In 1812, after being destroyed by an earthquake, the mission was rebuilt along a straight line to provide a quicker evacuation route.

Vivian pointed out the mission's central theme of resurrection in the face of so many tragedies.

La Purísima, we had read, was the eleventh mission established in the state. Restored to its original appearance in 1951, sitting on 966 acres near the central coast of California, the state park features the ancient, weatherworn tools of survival in a harsh and often hostile environment: the iron of kettles and anvils, the baked clay of aqueducts, the stone and adobe of walls, the yoke of oxen and ethnicity, the icon and burning wax of sustained devotion. In adjoining rooms were cock-and-flint rifles and floorboards worn by prayer. Protection had always been hard-won.

We toured the grounds and they were lovely. After we finished, Vivian insisted on climbing a hill near the exit. It was a long climb uphill through the sand, but we enjoyed the lovely fragrance of wildflowers along the way. It was beautiful—we could look over the valleys in all directions and to the ocean. About a quarter of the way up, Vivian needed to stop to catch her breath.

"Vivian," I had told her, "you don't have to do this. You are exhausted." Maybe it was the sweat fogging my eyeglasses, but I still could not see what was driving her. Vivian was determined, steely in her desire. A hard and dry wind whipped our hair. When Vivian stopped every few steps, I wiped the hair from her eyes.

"Are you sure you want to do this, honey? We don't need to go so far to get a view."

When the path bent sharply to our left and steeply inclined, I finally saw what she had seen from the beginning: Rising from the top of the hill stood a large wooden cross.

I wondered how I could have missed it. Rising some thirty feet out of sandy dirt, it was rough and hewn with initials. When we arrived at its base driven into concrete, Vivian asked for time to be alone. I walked to a railing forming a half circle around the cross and could see the mountains in the distance, layer upon layer. Ocean mists had settled there. I thought about all that Vivian had already been through. For a few minutes, I prayed for her.

When I turned around, I saw my wife clinging to the cross. Slowly, along a semicircle of fence, I walked. I wanted to see her face. From my perspective, it was hidden and cradled by her left arm; a scorching wind blew her hair across my field of vision. Circling slowly, I saw her lips moving in prayer—silently and rapidly.

Therefore, strengthen your feeble arms and weak knees. Circling slowly, I saw her frock—so delicate with pastels and flowers—whip against the cross. The sound of it seemed so urgent. *Make level paths for your feet, so that the lame may not be disabled, but rather healed.* Slowly circling, circling, searching for her eyes, I could see she was crying. I noticed the sleeve of her blouse tear-stained. *But for you who revere my name, the sun of righteousness will rise with healing in its wings.* I finally saw her full face—pleading, eyes closed, and filled with a mix of expectation, disappointment, hope, and longing. Silently circling, I lost track of time. I was absorbed in my wife's dependence, her clinging to the cross. It may have taken me ten minutes to complete the railing's semicircle, calling again for my wife. It may have been an hour. I tried my voice against the gusting wind: "Vivian, sweetheart, Vivian, sweetheart . . ."

I walked toward her.

She stood, leaning on the cross, and lifted a prayer she would later record in her journal.

> *Jesus, I cling to your cross—if this is my cross let me take it joyfully and be worthy of the cross you have chosen for me.*

When I put my arm around her waist, she released her grip from the cross, like someone falling, and I caught her against my chest.

Walking down to the parking lot, I nearly had to carry her. Several others, winding toward the cross, asked if they could help. I politely refused. I was convinced we would make it back safely together.

It seemed I could see so far, and was so close to God. Thank you, Lord, for the privilege of being there with you at your cross.

✦ ✦ ✦

In Cambria, near the Fog Catcher Inn on Moonstone Drive, the sea lions bawled at a crescent and sinking sun. At twilight, Vivian and I lit a fire. I started to read the verses we had recorded on the three-by-five cards. When I came to Psalm 91:14-16, I personalized it for her.

> "Because she loves me," says the Lord, "I will rescue her; I will protect her, for she acknowledges my name. She will call upon me, and I will answer her; I will be with her in trouble, I will deliver her and honor her. With long life will I satisfy her and show her my salvation."

Before I had finished, my wife gave me a gentle smile. She could see I was struggling to read the cards by the low and flickering light of our fire.

Vivian was deepening her studies in the grace of seeing with the eyes of faith.

THE GRACE
OF DEPENDENCE

7 BEAUTY AND THE BEAST

Melissa was with her mother as she wrote the side effects of chemotherapy into one of her journals.

Chemotherapy–

Days 1–3

   Nausea

   Coated tongue + foaming mouth

   Chemical smell + taste

   Exhaustion

Days following

   Queasiness + lack of appetite

   Constipation

   Hair loss

   Watery eyes + runny nose

   Mouth + tongue sores

   Slight temperature

Sweating + chilling
Bumps on skin
Flat red bumps and brown scales
Increased exhaustion

Purposely scheduled to conclude before April 19, 1997—the day of her daughter's wedding—Vivian was determined to limit the disruption of her chemotherapy. While anticipating her wedding day, Melissa also understood her mother's fear.

I am totally terrified by the thought of chemotherapy.
I don't want the pain and nausea and the poison
coursing through all my veins and to every organ
of my body. I don't want my hair to fall out.

Sitting next to her mother, Melissa listened as the doctor explained the most serious side effect—short- and long-term damage to the body's immune system. Because bone marrow cells, which generate red and white blood cells, are fast growing, they are also vulnerable to toxicity. While chemotherapy kills cancer cells, the toxins also damage some of the body's greatest weapons for fighting its own war. The idea, the doctor told them, was to kill off enough cancer cells so the body's own defenses, not too greatly wounded, would destroy the rest. For chemotherapy to help win the war, doctors have to carefully calculate casualty rates of good and bad cells.

There in the doctor's office, Melissa heard her mother tell the "joke" for the first time: "It sounds like a cure that kills."

In addition to the physical damage, Melissa understood chemotherapy's damage to her mother's emotions. Hair cells, which also rapidly divide, are killed by the toxins. Although Vivian never told her, Melissa knew how much her mother dreaded baldness. From some of her earliest memories, Melissa admired the way Vivian occupied her beauty, the seemingly effortless manner in which she presented and carried herself. For her mother to be bald threatened a stripping of more than outward beauty.

In between chemotherapy treatments, mother and daughter went shopping from town to town to town, from the Queen Mary Bridal Extravaganza to Costa Mesa through San Fernando Valley and back again.

59

Together, they shared a vision of how perfect the wedding day would be: a white church on a mountain overlooking a blue ocean.

Together, they joked about how they could never find the Mon Ami, a bridal shop just a few miles from where we lived, without getting badly lost.

Together, they made their plans for coming days: a reception by a harbor with dolphins leaping in the distance, a party on a porch at night, walks on the beach with a cup of coffee and good friends.

Together, in their collective mind's eye, mother and daughter had it all pictured perfectly.

✦ ✦ ✦

Melissa remembers one particular afternoon after a morning of shopping for wedding shoes and another session of chemotherapy. After her mother had decided to relax in a warm bath, Melissa heard a wailing scream. When she raced down the hall and knocked on the bathroom door, she waited a few moments for a response. Hearing none, she bolted through the door.

Standing behind her mother, Melissa could see Vivian's shoulders in motion—she was weeping violently. She watched as her mother pulled out clumps of hair, her hands in frantic rhythm. Melissa looked down into the bathtub; she could hardly see the water—her mother's hair covered almost the entire surface. When Melissa was finally able to hold the gaze of her mother's eyes, she knew she would never forget the look of terror. Until her sobbing subsided many minutes later, Melissa held her gently.

60

A day after losing her hair, Vivian recorded some glimpses of God's goodness in her thanksgiving journal:

- *Your grace as my hair fell out.*
- *That it fell out quickly.*
- *That I had Melissa here.*
- *That I had the courage to wear a scarf this morning and go out in public.*

On that blistering hot day, mother and daughter once again got lost on the way to the bridal shop. They laughed and laughed, and Melissa told her mother how good she looked in her blue scarf.

Melissa and I dressed and went to Fenderbender's and met Richard for lunch. Then we bought the cushion, garter, and Mel's shoes at the bridal shop and I came home and I changed my scarf. There was a message from Mary at the Positive Image Center saying that my wig had arrived. So we went over to the City of Hope and picked it up. It looked so cute I kept it on for my appointment with Dr. Wagman.

That evening, after Vivian had recovered from a bout of nausea, they went out to dinner and resumed their wedding plans: white roses on twin arbors, gentle lace and trim, family and friends, and toasts to everlasting happiness.

> *Melissa and I had dinner on the balcony at the Las Brisas—we watched the sun set over the Pacific. What a great day!*

While waiting for one of her afternoon chemotherapy appointments, Vivian shared with Melissa a verse God had given her, a verse that would become a metaphor for her battle with cancer. Reading from her journal, Vivian quoted Exodus 14:13-14:

> *Do not be afraid. Stand firm and you will see the deliverance the Lord will bring you today. The Egyptians you see today you will never see again. The Lord will fight for you; you need only to be still.*

As she sat with her daughter, Vivian wrote in her journal:

> *I am sitting in the chemotherapy room with the chemicals dripping into my blood. The red Adriamycin is the Red Sea that will inundate and bury and drown the Egyptians. They will be drowned forever—never to be seen again. The horse and the rider will both be thrown into the sea. Oh, Lord, wash away those Egyptians invading my body.*

Upon returning home, following a long siege of nausea, Vivian returned to her journal:

I came home and immediately began to feel sick. I could feel the massive die-off of the cells in my mouth already. They had been foaming a lot like foam from toothpaste. I went to bed for a few hours. I woke up and in an hour I began to vomit. It was awful.

A week after her last poison cocktail and a week before her daughter's wedding day, Vivian was exhausted. April 9 was a day full of taxes, alterations, traffic jams, layaways, pickups, construction zones, fittings, runarounds, dead ends, and the frenzied pressing of a thousand and one details.

In one of the day's few unrushed moments, mother and daughter, at the same moment and with the same inflection, both exclaimed: "Oh, how beautiful!" When Melissa tried on her wedding veil, they both knew it was perfect.

That night, in a restless exhaustion—a combination of the day's stresses and the remaining toxins—Vivian fell into a strange and unsettling dream.

I had a baby. It was a girl baby and Richard and I were delighted. For some reason, we left her inside the car all night by herself without changing her. The next morning, I got in and took off the soaking wet diaper. When we got home the baby ran naked out into the rain and got soaking wet. I went out to get her and also brought in a lamb. When I looked at the baby, I was delighted with her beautiful eyes—a blue green.

I knew Melissa would be delighted too.

I can only guess the baby is symbolic of the new me

I want to become. I still need to change; no one else can change me, I have to do it. I need cleansing. I invite the Lamb of God to do it. I have been praying for new eyes to see life with. I hope I am getting new eyes. Today I was very, very tired. I am at a low point in this cycle.

From now on everything should get better soon.

On her wedding day in the bride's room of a church overlooking the Pacific Ocean, Melissa remembers her mother helping her dress. When she was finished, she pulled the wedding veil from Melissa's face, caressed her cheek, and told her how beautiful she was.

63

Moments before the ceremony, Melissa watched as her mother nervously fiddled with her wig.

I hate my wig.

When she helped her mother adjust it, both of them smiling into the mirror, Melissa reminded her of a recent boast.

"You thought you were so cute when you first got it," she said.

Her mother told her a secret. She had come to believe she was rather good-looking bald. She had just lacked the necessary grace to see it before.

Walking together toward the church sanctuary, they laughed at that.

On her wedding day, nearly everyone commented on the continuing faith and beauty of Melissa's mother. Also radiant with joy, Melissa was quick to agree.

8 A TIME TO SOW

I had prepared our garden for planting. The dirt was tilled, water cans filled, and plants placed in careful lines. Vivian's gloves, sunglasses, knee pads, and spade awaited her. Kneeling in the shade of a grape arbor marking the entrance to our three-tiered garden, I noticed that neither the cancer nor the weeks of calculated poison had touched her beauty. She looked like a million bucks.

"I bought all of our favorites," I said to her.

Watching her eyes scan the rows of onions, basil, lettuce, peppers, thyme, horseradish, and cilantro, I could see the reflection of green in green. At that moment, the depth of her loveliness took my breath away. With a straw hat and a blue bandanna protecting her bald head from the California sun, she overturned the first dirt. We both smiled: Our long-standing tradition of planting a spring garden to-gether would continue.

The thirty-two years of our marriage we counted in springtimes, the consistent and cyclical rhythm of renewal. For each of us, working a spring garden was as necessary and self-forgetful as prayer. We both loved the feel of dirt in our hands, the blue of a bright sky, and the shared memories of our life together. When other certainties fell away, we found consolation and rebirth in the simplicity of planting side by side. Over the years, through God's faithfulness, we discovered we could always depend on a spring garden.

Vivian joked that our love possessed and enjoyed different sea-sons. For me, our love was a singular event of planning and plant-ing, a time to sow. For Vivian, planting marked the beginning of a process; she could envision the colors of harvest.

For both of us, planting renewed places deep in our souls. Easter was embedded in spring: the hope of life beginning anew. As I watched my wife dig into the earth, flushed and wasted by chemo-therapy, I wrapped one arm around her and, with the other, helped her shovel. After each plant, when I checked her eyes for fatigue, I realized that even in the face of cancer, she still possessed the power to startle me with her beauty.

In our spring garden bordered by pomegranates, azaleas, and filled with the scent of water poured over dirt, I held Vivian's hand. As we planted, slowly, side by side, we mostly worked the dirt in silence. I remembered when she had shown me the scar from her lumpectomy, a 2.5-inch incision on her left breast. I held her when she cried. I understood Vivian would certainly suffer. Yet, with a cultivated love, Vivian would remind me of the connection between pruning and harvest, and I would touch another scar and whisper of her continuing attractiveness. We were content to live with wounds.

But God could not take my wife. Just as surely as spring followed winter, in the continuing cycle of our intertwined lives, I had convinced myself we always would plant gardens together.

Lost in thought, I noticed my wife calling to me.

". . . Richard . . . Richard . . ."

I turned to her with a smile, attentively.

"Could you get me a drink of cold water?" She looked weak, her face flushed and pale at the same time. She had stopped planting.

"I would be happy to."

I told her to wait; I would be right back.

She assured me she had no plans to leave.

A few minutes later, I stood in the garden confused, holding a glass of water. Lying at my feet in the shade of the grape arbor were Vivian's gloves, sunglasses, knee pads, and spade. The instruments were discarded carefully, with calculated order, as if they had not been used. A plant lay halfway out of its container. A spilled pitcher traced a dark circle in the dirt. Vivian was gone.

Vivian was gone.

The thought bounced around my head like a trapped wasp. She was gone. My wife of thirty-two years was gone. Vivian was gone. My lover was gone. Spinning in a circle, as a red-edged panic moved along my nerves, I was pierced by the image of the gardening tools she had left behind. Vivian was gone. As hard as I tried to clear my mind of the thought so I could logically survey the situation, I was stung and stung again with a certainty: Vivian was gone.

God would take my wife.

In my confusion and anger, I screamed silently: *Lord, we do gardens* together!

Setting down Vivian's glass of water, I covered my face with my hands and wept.

"I don't plant gardens alone. Oh, God, please, please, please, we plant gardens together."

I don't know how long I cried. When I was finally able to compose myself, I saw Vivian's glass of water sitting on the table. I picked it up, stepped over the discarded gardening tools, and desperately scanned the horizon for the woman I loved.

✦ ✦ ✦

Walking from our garden to the back porch, having not yet fully recovered from my sense of panic, I noticed two things at once: the glass of water turning warm in my hand and Vivian lying on the lounge chair in the shade. Through my tears, I bent over to hug her. She noticed I was trembling. I saw her blue bandanna was tilted slightly to one side.

"I thought I had lost you," I said to her.

When she saw a remnant of terror in my eyes, she hugged me and told me, "I am right here."

Although I soon recovered my faith that Vivian would be healed, I never completely escaped the image of those discarded garden tools. Waking up in fear on a moonless night, or praying over her pain, or lost in the beauty of her smile, the picture would float into my mind's eye, spinning bright silver threads of panic and loss. In a spring garden, lost and alone amidst the litter of what she left behind, I understood I would never be able to plant alone.

There is a time to sow and a time to reap, and I could not face the thought of Vivian's presence with me in one season and absence from me in another.

9 A COSTLY
HARVEST

That spring, Vivian had a dream about a house. In the journal recording the event, she wrote:

> As long as I can remember, I have been having dreams about houses. It used to be that all the houses were big and scary. Frequently, I would be looking for a place to hide. Sometimes I would be trying to get away from something scary that was pursuing me. Sometimes I would crawl into a tiny space in a chest or crawl through a really tiny hole to get into another room.

Yet this dream was starkly different. Where the houses in the other dreams had caused her to feel claustrophobic, this house was ever expanding. Vivian was standing in the basement, wrestling with the question of why. Why was she standing in a basement, and why had she put her children to bed here? Why were her children little again? Why was her sister's family also in this home? When she looked up, she was surprised by a room opening up.

> *I was seeing a large and wonderful room with rock walls and decorated in lodge style. Even though I was standing in a basement, it was flooded with light. Then I looked up, and there was a huge skylight and window well. It was a wonderful room and I was delighted. Then I looked at the end of the room and there was another, even larger room opening up. It was very richly furnished with beautiful wall hangings and upholsteries and dressing tables and plush sofas.*

As the rooms progressively appeared before her eyes, one springing from another, each larger and more elegant than the last, Vivian experienced awe and overwhelming delight.

> *I was so amazed and pleased that I had these rooms and didn't even know it.*

The French doors were particularly striking. She walked toward a wonderful river of light flowing through their panes and cracks. When she opened the doors, she was flooded with a stream of velvet white, which was also warm. She wanted to stay there forever. It was as if light were a thing to be felt as well as seen.

72

In this dream, I found that the house had new, lovely, comfortable rooms, each opening to an even more lovely space.

The final room opened up into a garden. She was in the basement again, impossibly. As white and warm light fell from skylights, she walked into a garden room and saw a beauty that took her breath away: pomegranates, oranges, apples, peaches, grapes. They were ripe, heavy and moist with seed. How, she wondered, does fruit grow in a cellar? Her first inclination was to build a wall around the garden, to protect such fragile fecundity. Suddenly, she felt the rude invasion of fear.

73

There was the smell of threat.

The appearance of beauty, she understood, was up for grabs. Suffering was the only certain reality.

When I looked again, the fruit was gone, and I noticed the garden was not yet finished. It made me feel sad. There was still much work to be done.

Building a wall would keep her from what she needed to do, and she understood the harvest of such lovely fruit to be worth whatever risk. She awoke with this understanding: By God's grace, she could face any real and lurking danger.

THE GRACE
OF SURRENDER

10 AFTER THESE THINGS

During the season of Lent, Vivian was reminded of the birth of ancient Israel.

> *It is my goal to carefully read through the whole Bible. I have been reading in Genesis. I love the stories of Creation, Adam and Eve, Noah, Abraham, Isaac, Jacob, and Joseph.*

Through the reality of her own experience, Vivian noted the distance—in time, space, and energy—between Abraham's calling and Moses standing on the border of the Promised Land, not permitted to enter. Waiting for the fulfillment of God's promise she understood to be a most difficult matter. Caught in the jaws of suffering and uncertainty, each of the patriarchs of faith was tempted to wonder: Is the deal still on?

Following another chemotherapy treatment, Vivian was sick and tired and filled with doubt. She vomited repeatedly and went to bed. She woke up, ate watery green Jell-O, vomited repeatedly again, and went back to bed. She could not help but wonder: *God, is the deal still on?* Not given to complaint or self-pity, she wrestled with despair in the pages of her journal.

> *Today, I am tired of being sick. I am tired of feeling tired and I am tired of having nothing to do and not feeling like doing anything. I am tired of feeling pain and nausea and illness. I'm tired of the ringing in my ears. I'm tired of going to the hospital and waiting for someone to poke me or photograph me or tell me more bad news.*
>
> *Lord, I'm sorry. I'm sorry for my life. I am sorry I have wasted so much of it by not doing anything good or worthwhile. I am sorry for investing so much of my energy into daydreaming and vanity. And I'm sorry for feeling sorry for myself. Lord, you promised to give strength to the weak, energy to the weary, hope to the downtrodden, and joy to the sorrowing. I wait upon you, Lord.*

On Good Friday, Vivian watched a televised sermon by Jack Hayford on the transitional event of Abraham's circumcision. Starting with the original promise of God, Dr. Hayford quoted Genesis 12:1-3:

> Now the Lord had said unto Abram, Get thee out of thy country, and from thy kindred, and from thy father's house, unto a land that I will shew thee: And I will make of thee a great nation, and I will bless thee, and make thy name

great; and thou shalt be a blessing: And I will bless them that bless thee, and curse him that curseth thee: and in thee shall all families of the earth be blessed. (KJV)

Dr. Hayford then fast-forwarded nearly a decade into Abram's life. He read from Genesis 15:1-3:

> After these things the word of the Lord came unto Abram in a vision, saying, Fear not, Abram: I am thy shield, and thy exceeding great reward. And Abram said, Lord God, what wilt thou give me, seeing I go childless. . . . Behold, to me thou hast given no seed: and, lo, [a servant] born in my house is mine heir. (KJV)

79

"After these things," Dr. Hayford said, was more than a literary transition, but a phrase filled with heartache. Having left his country—all that was familiar and comfortable—Abram could not be blamed if the Promised Land seemed farther away than when he began. Promised to be the "father of many nations," Abram and his wife, Sarai, were geriatric. Through a womb as dry as the desert they wandered in, how could they hope to multiply God's promise? Between promise and fulfillment, Abram wondered if the deal was still on *after these things:*

- ♦ a journey into wastelands toward an unspecified destination
- ♦ arrival to the Promised Land only to discover it was already possessed by the powerful Canaanites
- ♦ a detour to Egypt where, through Abram's cowardly deception, his wife joined the pharaoh's harem

- a family feud involving material goods
- the capture of his nephew and an armed battle for his rescue
- a test of Abram's life economies by the high priest Melchizedek

When Abram despaired through years of difficult waiting, God reappeared, gently and powerfully reminding him that he had missed the point. Dr. Hayford picked up the conversation in Genesis 15:4-5:

> And, behold, the word of the Lord came unto him, saying, This shall not be thine heir; but he that shall come forth out of thine own bowels shall be thine heir. And he brought him forth abroad, and said, Look now toward heaven, and tell the stars, if thou be able to number them: and he said unto him, So shall thy seed be. (KJV)

Abram's doubt required a new perspective. Away from walls and ceiling, under the unlimited majesty of a night sky while counting an eternity of stars, Abram was reminded of the power and love of God. In faith, in a hope against wildest hope, Abram chose to continue to believe in the sovereign care of God.

More than seven years earlier, Vivian had prayed for God to take her to another level of devotion. She had heard God saying he would, and she believed she was being called to a healing ministry. The year before she was diagnosed with cancer, Vivian had asked God to be a little more clear about her calling. All she could hear of his response was "trust me."

On the day marking the death of the Son of God, she found it difficult to see past her cancer and the medical community's grave warnings to the eventual fulfillment of God's promise. After these things—sickness, pain, and threat—she wrestled with the idea that she had somehow fumbled God's upward calling. Whom else did she have to blame? God certainly was not at fault.

Through the words of Dr. Hayford's sermon, she was transported to a seat under a clear night sky. *Count the stars if you can.* With the same power and love God used to set the stars in space, Vivian believed he would fulfill his promises.

✦ ✦ ✦

Years and years after God asked Abram to count the night stars, shortly after he turned ninety-nine, his wife remained as barren as an Egyptian tomb. Again God appeared with words of reassurance. Dr. Hayford quoted Genesis 17:1-6:

> The Lord appeared to Abram, and said unto him, I am the Almighty God; walk before me, and be thou perfect. And I will make my covenant between me and thee, and will multiply thee exceedingly. And Abram fell on his face: and God talked with him, saying, As for me, behold, my covenant is with thee, and thou shalt be a father of many nations. Neither shall thy name any more be called Abram, but thy name shall be Abraham; for a father of many nations have I made thee. And I will make thee exceeding fruitful. (KJV)

As an external sign of the covenant established by God, Abraham was circumcised.

In her journal notes of Dr. Hayford's sermon, Vivian included the New Testament application of circumcision as recorded in Colossians 2:9-12.

> *For in Christ all the fullness of the Deity lives in bodily form, and you have been given fullness in Christ, who is the head over every power and authority. In him you were also circumcised, in the putting off of the sinful nature, not with a circumcision done by the hands of men but with the circumcision done by Christ, having been buried with him in baptism and raised with him through your faith in the power of God, who raised him from the dead.*

82

Resurrecting a new perspective, Vivian equated the cutting away of circumcision to a gardener's work of pruning.

> *So this is my year for circumcision. I have prayed so long for God to give me a ministry. I prayed all last fall and winter for the Lord to prune and use me. I guess I did not imagine that the Lord would take me so literally. So now I have a large section of my left breast missing and a chunk missing out of my armpit. But I rejoice that this is a physical sign of my inward and spiritual pruning.*

When the things that are dear to us are stripped away, we have an opportunity to let go of our own vision of life and accept what God is doing in our lives. Learning the grace of surrender is costly, and it exacted from Vivian a terrible price. But it is a sure path to the power and love of God, which have a way of eclipsing those things we thought we couldn't live without.

11 STRENGTHENED BY LOVE

By the end of May, Vivian was feeling better. The poison of chemotherapy was abating. A modest healing service, with elders praying, had just been held. A miracle was in the process of sprouting. This is what we all believed.

With other members of the Azusa Pacific University board, we departed on a weeklong cruise to Alaska. We saw glaciers, eagles, and snowcapped peaks against blue skies. We rode a narrow-gauge railroad through a winding pass to the Yukon. We marveled at the land's beauty. We celebrated the majesty of our God. We had fun.

As another Southern California summer heated up, Vivian continued to feel that healing was occurring. In late August we celebrated our thirty-third anniversary.

✦ ✦ ✦

I remember the first time I fell under the spell of Vivian's beauty. Playing first base for my church softball team one summer, I noticed a blue convertible pull into the parking lot behind our team's bleachers. In the passenger's seat sat a woman I couldn't take my eyes off of. The sun was pooling in Vivian's hair.

All I can remember thinking was MY, MY, MY, MY, MY.

I played the remaining innings in a daze. After the game, I made it a point to tell my teammate Don how well he had played. "Thanks," he said. "Oh, this is Vivian, my sister-in-law." I said hi and we talked for a while. I can still remember the way her green eyes caught the light. I was smitten.

From a friend, I borrowed a copy of Olivet Nazarene's yearbook from the previous year. With some small guilt, at the age of twenty-three, I paged back through the seniors, the juniors, the sophomores, to the freshmen. My fingers traced the names and my eyes scanned the pictures. Baumgardner . . . Dilling . . . Lewis . . . Manning . . . Penn . . . Randall . . . Schmidt . . . Sloan . . . Snyder . . . Stray.

Stray, Vivian.

Vivian Stray. There she was. She was beautiful.

I still vividly recall my decision to ask her out on a date. Determined to meet her again, I drove from my apartment to Olivet Nazarene College, where Vivian was a sophomore. In my red 1961 Chevrolet Impala convertible, I cruised the campus hoping to "accidentally" run into her. On my second pass, in my rearview mirror I saw Vivian walking near the library with some of her friends. Once again, I was startled: MY, MY, MY. But the campus circle was a one-way street, and by the time I made it back to the spot where I had seen her, she had disappeared.

After reluctantly retracing the miles back to my apartment, I risked dialing her number: "Hello, Vivian, my name is Richard Felix. You probably don't remember me, but I played first base at one of your brother-in-law's softball games last summer." I swallowed so hard I was sure she heard it.

"Oh, I know who you are," she said.

MY, MY, MY.

"You do?" I choked out.

"Sure, you drove your car away barefooted . . . no shoes!"

While my pulse raced in my ears, we chatted. Eventually I got to my main point.

"Could I take you to church next Wednesday?" I asked. "Maybe we could get a bite to eat after."

"Sure."

When I hung up, I ran racing through the long halls of the home I shared with two other bachelors, shouting, "She's beautiful! She's beautiful! She's beautiful!" When my friends, looking alarmed and concerned, asked me to explain, I repeated myself. "She's beautiful!" It was all I could think to say. Inside, I felt like the bright blue of a Laguna Beach spring sky.

Almost immediately, I knew I needed Vivian. In her presence, I had the sense of completion, a soft and buoyant feeling of filling up. She experienced the same understanding. Vivian and I were enraptured by what each of us lacked. I was enthralled with her exotic Oriental beauty (she was the daughter of a Chinese doctor and an American missionary), and she was charmed with my penchant for making the most of any circumstance. On our second date, en route to a Nat King Cole concert, I managed to run a red light in the fever of anticipation. The campus police pulled us over. I told Vivian to leave it to me. After I smoothly talked my way out of a ticket, I saw she was impressed. I was cool under fire.

We both loved Nat King Cole. That evening, listening to his bright-blue-sky voice in the lyrics to "Unforgettable," we held hands for the first time.

Following a short romance, convinced by a reality of complete-ness, Vivian and I married ten months after our first date.

✦ ✦ ✦

On that August evening as we celebrated thirty-three years of marriage by packing a picnic and renting a pontoon boat, we drifted quietly across an alpine lake cooled by gentle breezes. Over water still as glass, evening slipped into night. We spoke of our continuing love.

If a war against a terrible disease can have a good time, this was it. So many prayers had been lifted and we believed a good God hears the cries of those who love him. Buoyed by what seemed to be the momentum of miracle, we were determined to move for-ward with our lives. In some mysterious fashion, we understood the wisdom of adversity—both in marriage and faith—and be-lieved the cancer, having been driven finally into the Red Sea, would serve to make us stronger.

For our anniversary I asked a jeweler to cut a heart-shaped pen-dant in half. One half was shaped into an R and the other half into a V. In joining the R and the V, one heart was created. I intended the necklaces as a symbolic image of our forever love. By God's grace, we would emerge together better than before.

We had decided to celebrate our wedding anniversary at Lake Arrowhead during a working vacation. On loan to us from a neighbor whose wife had also battled cancer, the house where we stayed was perfect for planning, resting, and anticipating what God was about to do. A new school year at APU—its one hundredth anniversary—was about to begin. With a view of the lake, we prepared together mostly in a wonderful silence. I composed two critical speeches—for the annual opening chapel and the faculty-staff banquet. With the courage my wife had shown, I wanted to encourage the school to cling to the cross. Vivian also prepared to communicate her experience with cancer to the student body during a chapel service in mid-September.

From a balcony overlooking the lake, we prayed together each morning, asking God to bless our efforts. Far from a death sentence, we viewed Vivian's cancer as having the potential to multiply ministry. We talked of the year ahead, and we agreed change was the one certainty. After just having endured radiation and two sessions of chemotherapy, Vivian cherished the cool and still air. During our four days at Lake Arrowhead, Vivian rested in the fact that God is good and the creator of such breathtaking beauty.

On the morning of our anniversary, Vivian woke up and told me she dreamed of Kotare cranes. That was good, she said; they were Chinese symbols for long life.

That night we toasted our love life.

"To another year together."

"To another year together."

In the fading light I explained how our two necklaces—one

with the R and the other the V—were designed to fit together and form one heart.

In God's merciful providence, we do not know what lies ahead and for what purposes we are being strengthened.

12 STANDING
FIRM

At the end of October, Vivian found another lump—on her other breast.

> *Of course I am very much afraid. What else could it be but cancer? I have never had swollen lymph nodes for any illness. This lump is hard and irregular-shaped. It is unusual though for it to be on the opposite arm. When I begin to get paranoid, I think I have cancer everywhere in my body—a dry cough is lung cancer, constant headaches mean a brain tumor, aching joints mean bone cancer. Who knows? The problem with metastatic breast cancer is there is no way to find out it has metastasized until it is so serious a cure is no longer likely.*

On the way to the City of Hope to have her second breast lump examined, Vivian had every reason to fear. Yet on the border of panic, she found an unexpected calm.

> *On the drive to the City of Hope—somewhere between leaving the house where I was in tears and arriving at the hospital—I gained a great peace and sense of God's presence. I did not see how that was possible.*

Dr. Wagman, in his kindly manner, examined the lymph node carefully.

> *He said it was a lymph node about one centimeter in diameter, palpable, freestanding. He told me he wanted to see it again in another month. On the way home, I told myself I will cling to the verse the Lord had given me: "Do not be afraid. Stand firm and you will see the deliverance the Lord will bring you today. The Lord will fight for you; you need only to be still."*

Three days before Thanksgiving, Vivian returned for her follow-up. The hard node was still there. The next day, with Vivian under general anesthesia, Dr. Wagman performed a biopsy. We waited for the results over Thanksgiving.

On December 5, in a meeting with Dr. Wagman and Dr. Leong, we were told the tumor was malignant. For the lump to have been found in the opposite breast puzzled both doctors. They wanted to do another battery of tests to determine if it represented a new cancer or a metastasis.

On December 10, Vivian received a devastating new diagnosis: recurrent inflammatory breast cancer.

> *We were told that the original cancer had mutated into an aggressive and fast-growing inflammatory cancer. Rather than growing as a tumor, inflammatory breast cancer grows like a net of fingerlike strands penetrating all through the tissue and appearing in the skin as red blotches and lumps. It is unnerving to watch it grow daily.*
>
> *I was told that my case is highly atypical. At the City of Hope, they have only seen two other cases of recurrent cancer appearing as inflammatory cancer.*
>
> *A rigorous treatment plan was recommended: more chemotherapy, a double mastectomy, extensive radiation, and a bone marrow transplant.*

Because of the rare and voracious nature of recurrent inflammatory breast cancer, the City of Hope encouraged us to get another opinion. Fortunately, I was able to make an appointment with Dr. John Glaspy, medical director of the Bowyer Surgical Oncology Center. As part of the UCLA Medical Center, Glaspy—a round-faced, gentle-looking man whose tie is often crooked—rates as one of a handful of doctors at the forefront of cancer treatment and research.

In preparation for our meeting, Dr. Glaspy had reviewed Vivian's medical records, biopsy reports, and even a few specimen slides under a microscope. He understood what we were dealing with. When Vivian and I entered his office a few days before Christmas, he asked to speak with me alone first. From a door in his office, we walked out into an atrium filled with palm trees, sculptures, and plants. Beautifully landscaped, precisely engineered with bricks and gardens, the courtyard was designed to relieve pressures. Dr. Glaspy put his arm around me, and we walked slowly in a circle.

After he prefaced his remarks with "No one can ever be certain about these things," he reeled off a terrible prognosis.

The cancer would quickly kill my wife. He had seen this kind of cancer before.

"The problem of treating it," Dr. Glaspy told me, his arm still around me, "is that you simply end up cutting off an appendage and never get at the underlying issue."

With what revealed itself to be a deadly accurate prognosis, in a certain and staccato fashion, he told me what would happen to Vivian.

"She will first have more chemotherapy. Doctors will experiment with different combinations, but this will fail and the cancer will continue to spread."

His words possessed the rhythm of a clock ticking out the seconds.

"You must do whatever you can, so Vivian will have a double mastectomy, and within a short time, another biopsy will reveal that the cancer has spread further."

Walking around the atrium outside of his office, he wanted us to know: Time was a precious commodity. Inflammatory breast cancer with metastasis is rare and more rarely cured.

"Vivian will then undergo high-dose chemotherapy with peripheral stem cell rescue. More commonly, this is called a bone marrow transplant. We will take your wife as near to death as possible and use harvested stem cells to resurrect her. With a successful attempt to maintain a sanitized environment, Vivian will be spared any infection, which her hopefully recovering immune system would be helpless to eradicate.

"Within a short time the cancer will spread to her kidneys, liver, and/or brain. Vivian will have radiation. And the cancer will continue to spread.

"In the end, Vivian will die in one of three ways—a brain tumor, a liver shutdown, or by drowning in her lungs' own fluids."

My mind focused on how he was repeating himself: *And the cancer will continue to spread*.

We paused, and we looked each other in the eyes.

93

"How long?" I asked.

"A year, maybe two. The longest anyone has lived with this form of cancer is maybe four years."

I told him about our great faith.

He told me we were going to need it.

"For Vivian to be cured it is going to take a miracle," he said.

I told him about the thousands of people who were praying for just such a thing.

He apologized for having to be so blunt.

I said I understood.

We walked back into his office, and I could tell by Vivian's face she already comprehended what I would tell her when we returned home.

Richard and I went to see Dr. John Glaspy at the UCLA
Medical Center. He terrified me. He told us I have cancer
cells everywhere in my body—lungs, liver, blood—and my
chances, even with high-dose chemotherapy with stem cell

rescue, are optimistically less than 20 percent. So, here I am—with good odds I will not survive.

Lord, you know and number my days. There is nothing hidden from you. Help me to place all my faith in you, Lord. I love you and I long to see you face-to-face—but I want to do more things yet here and I want to pray my grandchildren through high school. Lord God, have mercy. I am just now learning how to love you and how to live for you. Have mercy. Hear my cry. Come to me. Touch me. Heal me. Love me. Help me to stand firm.

2 Cor. 1:21-22: "Now it is God who makes both us and you stand firm in Christ. He anointed us, set his seal of ownership on us, and put his Spirit in our hearts as a deposit, guaranteeing what is to come."

After this pair of terrible diagnoses, we took a trip to Wichita to begin an experimental treatment. To break up an eighteen-hour drive between Southern California and western Kansas, we stopped to rest in the mountains of Utah. Although I would not know it until reading her journals following her death, Vivian powerfully experienced God along the way.

I am incredibly privileged to have had a glimpse of you in Utah. How can I doubt your infinite power and majesty? I also thank you for showing me that your peace is always there, but I have to allow it to rule my heart. My own dwelling on the future and my fear drive the peace away.

Vivian recorded her moment of insight by borrowing the words of her favorite poet, Gerard Manley Hopkins:

> *The world is charged with the grandeur of God.*
> *It will flame out, like shining from shook foil.*

Over time, Vivian began to see—again in the poet's words—"the dearest freshness deep down things." Vivian could perceive the faint but radiant lines of God's fingerprints, even through the dark lenses of pain and suffering.

> *When everything else is taken away from us, God remains.*
> *Without other distractions, we begin to see him more clearly.*

95

In her two remaining references to her experience with God in the mountains of Utah, she wrote:

> *I saw you leaping and skipping with joy on the mountaintop.*
> *I saw you in the mountains, tall and beautiful, skipping and*
> *leaping.*

THE GRACE
OF GRATITUDE

13 THE QUESTION
OF A GREATER MIRACLE

When Vivian prayed for healing, which she initially did with great frequency and urgency, she was never simply thinking of her body alone. Six months after her first diagnosis, she was asked to speak at a student chapel with Gordon Coulter, an APU professor who was also battling cancer. Together, they examined Jesus' probing question to a paralytic recorded in John 5:6 (NKJV): "Do you want to be made well?"

Gordon sat on the stage as chapel began, amazed by his sweaty palms. In his combined fifty years as pastor and professor, he could not recall such severe speaking anxiety. It felt more like a case of wasps than butterflies.

His speaking confidence, in fact, was why Vivian had agreed to help him share the experiences of cancer with the students. Gordon had assured her he could handle the majority of the chapel time. As he and Vivian, holding a box, reached the podium, Gordon sipped a cup of water. He hoped no one could see his hands shaking.

"This is probably the most difficult talk I have ever given at APU," Gordon began. "On July 13, I was diagnosed with a lymph-node cancer called lymphoma. I've never been seriously ill before. I'm currently in chemo and I have my treatments in series of three-week periods. Fifty percent of the people with my form of cancer are healed. Fifty percent are not."

Opening his Bible, Gordon began reading the story of the para-lytic recorded in John 5:1-6.

> After this there was a feast of the Jews, and Jesus went
> up to Jerusalem. Now there is in Jerusalem by the
> Sheep Gate a pool, which is called in Hebrew, Bethesda,
> having five porches. In these lay a great multitude of sick
> people, blind, lame, paralyzed, waiting for the moving
> of the water. For an angel went down at a certain time
> into the pool and stirred up the water; then whoever
> stepped in first, after the stirring of the water, was made
> well of whatever disease he had. Now a certain man was
> there who had an infirmity thirty-eight years. When Jesus
> saw him lying there, and knew that he already had been in
> that condition a long time, He said to him, "Do you want
> to be made well?" (NKJV)

He looked up from his Bible and continued speaking to the thousand-plus students sitting in front of him.

"Everyone in the area had heard of Jesus' healings. Everyone wanted to get close to him. On this particular day the scene was set near the Temple, which was bordered by the pool—a large area about the size of three football fields. At any given moment, more than a thousand invalids waited for the angel to come and trouble the water. Actually, the pool was probably a pocket in the earth emitting gases. It was quite a sight. People were pushing and shoving to beat each other to the water.

"It was no accident that Jesus showed up at the pool that day. Jesus wandered through the crowd and found the paralyzed man. After being told he had been lying there for thirty-eight years unable to move into the troubled waters, Jesus asked him a haunting question: 'Do you want to be made well?'"

Reaching to take another sip of water, Gordon looked out over the sea of students. Suddenly, he began to laugh. "I notice that some of you guys have your heads shaved for me. That is truly a source of inspiration." He moved from his laughter to what he wanted to say.

"As Vivian and I prepared for this chapel, we had to ask ourselves that question again and again: 'Do you want to be made well?'"

✦ ✦ ✦

Following weeks of preparation for their talk, Vivian had been the one to suggest carrying along a Pandora's box. Cancer, they both agreed, was a lot like that. Out of the same earthy place came such vivid terror and delicate hope.

In deciding what to tell students about living with cancer, Vivian and Gordon became friends. She confessed to Gordon the need for a deeper healing than simply physical. The diagnosis of her cancer had exposed unresolved issues in her life, such as patterns of perfectionism and control. Through her suffering, God was changing her. She was in the process of becoming a different person. Gordon revealed a similar movement of God in his own life. The greatest curse and blessing of cancer, they agreed, was the shattering of the illusion of control. For both of them, the future was wrapped up in faith, and present moments were increasingly full of a grace inexplicably more than equal to the horror. But they also shared a desperate desire to live. While praying fervently for each other's physical healing, they also asked for courage to hold out for a greater miracle.

102

✦ ✦ ✦

Finally unleashed from his nerves, Gordon repeated the question to the students:

"Do you want to be made well? Do you want to be made well? That question addresses something much larger than if we have cancer or not. It's much bigger than the physical. The paralytic got a miracle in an instant. And that's what we so often want from God—a miracle vending machine where we put a prayer in the slot and out zaps an answer. More often, a miracle does not happen that way. God often walks us through a journey. Sometimes the destination is irrelevant. It's what you learn on the journey that's valuable.

"As we prepared for this chapel, the running joke between Vivian and me was: 'What's the worst that could happen to us? We could go to heaven. We could get healed physically—we fervently pray so every day.' But maybe the secret to most miracles is in learning to ask 'What?' and not 'Why?' 'Why?' is the most natural question. 'What?' is the much tougher and more profitable question: 'What, God, do you have for me as I'm going through this situation?'"

As they had planned, Gordon closed with a fable about a three-legged dog redeemed by a boy wearing leg braces. Grace, they knew, was like that: inhabiting the strangest places. Before making his final point, Gordon stood in an extended silence.

"I stand before you today to tell you, even if I do not live many more years, I would not exchange a guaranteed cure for what I have learned and how I have been touched along the way."

Vivian had researched ancient mythology for her portion of the presentation. Pandora had been the first woman created, according to the mythmakers. At her creation, each of the gods blessed her with a special present. After standing through a long and divine line, Aphrodite gave her beauty; Hermes, persuasion; and Apollo, music. She also was given a box that she was warned never to open. Into this box, each god had placed a terrible evil—suffering, sorrow, malignancy, revenge, envy, and various plagues.

Pandora possessed the best gifts, but she was also endowed with an insatiable and deadly curiosity. As a present to the earth and to man, Pandora came with divine blessings and a hankering for terrible knowledge. When she was overcome with curiosity and opened the box, she loosed a swarm of evils upon mankind.

Standing next to her friend through a shared adversity, Vivian began to speak. "Having cancer," she told the students, "is a lot like opening Pandora's box." She held up the box in her hands, took a deep breath, and continued with a shaky voice.

"Terrible things were coming out of the box. Not only cancer,

103

but a terrible cancer—one that metastasized and spread to other parts of my body. During the last eight months it has been cut, and I've undergone chemotherapy and radiation. There have been a lot of difficult days and difficult times."

Allowing the horror to wash over her, Pandora had dared to re-open the box. With great courage, she looked again and saw it empty—but for a white feather of a thing she named hope.

"But good things also came out of Pandora's box," Vivian continued, lifting the box once again. "This is the same box that was delivered to me on the day I was diagnosed with cancer. It was filled with your cards of prayer and encouragement. The love you have shown has given me hope.

"I have discovered the incredible unity in the body of Christ. The body rushed to support me. We were overwhelmed by prayers, flowers, and gifts. The Lord never gives a crown without a cross. And he never gives a cross without a crown. It is a crown of joy, and it is truly a greater miracle."

14 THE MYSTERY
OF WAITING

The Bible's lone definition of faith is in Hebrews 11:1: "Now faith is being sure of what we hope for and certain of what we do not see." During the onslaught of her cancer, Vivian prayed consistently for God to give her new eyes to see the larger—and largely invisible—realities. She longed for God to help her see from a higher perspective.

On the evening before her double mastectomy on April 2, 1998, Vivian stood in front of the full-length mirror and had trouble seeing beyond her own reflection.

> *I looked at my body. It looked really good for a fifty-three-year-old woman. My legs are thin and firm and I have no cellulite. My breasts are 36C and have no droop. I*

am very proud of my body and happy with the way I look. I mourned over my breasts. In a short time, I knew they would be gone and I will have gross scars across my chest. The worst thing is—my body will never be the same again.

On the morning of her surgery, Dr. Wagman used a felt marker to draw thin purple lines around my wife's breasts. A scalpel would soon follow those lines. Along with the other scars, Vivian joked her chest was beginning to look like a road map. In the overwhelmingly physical landscapes cancer moves a person through—the palpable and unrelenting realities of pain and loss—it is often difficult to see beyond the physical with the eyes of faith.

A few days before Easter, recovering in the hospital from a surgery that removed both her breasts, Vivian watched another televised sermon by Jack Hayford called "Kingdom Come Vision." The eyes of faith, Dr. Hayford said, attempt to focus on the world at the very points the invisible and slow-coming Kingdom of God intersect and overlap. He called such a place "a seam between the kingdoms."

The eyes of faith are focused on mystery. In the Greek written by Paul, the word translated as "mystery" does not share the precise meaning it has today, Dr. Hayford explained. In the original Greek, the word carries a connotation of a slow unveiling. What was once hidden is now *in the process of* being revealed. The emphasis is on discovery as much as search. Such mystery slowly—often painfully slowly—unfolds. In the canvas of humanity, God has to weave an eternity of souls and needs. If we fail to see with the eyes of faith, the mystery seems either to unravel, stall, or, worse, mutate. Because God exists in eternity, Dr. Hayford continued, we are tempted to despise waiting through the long days of our suffering. It is not surprising, then, that one of God's most frequent requests is to "wait on me."

To stand firm and wait on him.

Dr. Hayford illustrated a need to maintain an open perspective with an unusual painting hung in the gallery of a world-class art collector. Amid originals of Rembrandt and Van Gogh, the collector had prominently hung a picture that looked as if he had purchased it on an abandoned piece of Las Vegas property from the back of a pickup truck. Brushed with paint-by-number technique, a cousin to velvet Elvises, the painting was dreadful.

When asked why (which he frequently was), the art collector would smile and ask his own question: "Do you treasure a good mystery?"

Almost everyone said they did. The art collector asked them to stare into the painting, as bad as it seemed to be. Looking into the circular pigments of paint, those with eyes to see could eventually begin to discern another reality: emerging from a dark green jungle whipped by strong winds, a far different picture existed. The mystery required a certain perspective.

For many, the art collector reported, what had emerged was a white stallion charging.

Just as the picture seemed to paint a scene of being lost, so we often seem lost in the circumstances of our life. . . . Lord Jesus, give us eyes to see you as ever present, ever powerful.

107

✦ ✦ ✦

On the Saturday between Good Friday and Easter, Vivian came home from the hospital missing her breasts. For weeks, there were

no entries in her journals. When she wrote again, she asked forgiveness for being focused on her loss and pain.

> *My appearance is as one newly shorn. I have no breasts—*
> *only scars. I am tired and sore. Every time I try to move*
> *I have incredible pain. I have stitches—at least 35 to 45*
> *on either side of my chest. My chest is covered with lumps*
> *and swelling everywhere. Tubes and drains are hanging out*
> *of my body in five places. Both my arms ache constantly and*
> *my chest feels like a hundred fishhooks are piercing my skin.*
> *I look and feel like I have been in all the battle scenes of*
> *Braveheart.*
>
> *I haven't written for weeks. I am so sorry, Lord. Yesterday, I*
> *felt like I finally turned a corner on the severe pain and*
> *tightness. I pray for a fresh vision of you, my God. Help me to*
> *see you in all of your love and power. Transform me with a*
> *glimpse of who you really are. Do not let my gaze be fixed on*
> *anything but you.*

15 HARVESTING THE ETERNAL

In the spring of 1998, shaded from high-blue Southern Californian skies, our garden plants were abandoned for weeks. Sitting on the window ledge of our sunroom: basil, cherry tomatoes, head lettuce, thyme, onions, and asparagus. In the wake of Vivian returning home from the hospital after her double mastectomy, our spring tradition of planting a garden together stood in jeopardy.

I understood what was on the immediate horizon. A week after her surgery, the first test revealed the cancer to be still spreading. A bone marrow transplant—or, more accurately, high-dose chemotherapy with peripheral stem cell rescue (PSCR)—would soon follow. To plant our garden together, we had only a small window of time.

At Vivian's urging, I purchased the plants on a bright spring morning and unloaded them onto the window ledge on our back porch. Vivian was exhausted. Understanding what was ahead, I focused my attention on my wife's needs. In bed one evening Vivian and I designed a layout for the garden, but neither of us could find the heart or energy to turn the soil.

As the days slipped by, I convinced Vivian she needed her rest. In the most optimistic descriptions, high-dose chemotherapy was described by doctors as "harrowing" and "relentless." For those with metastatic cancer, like Vivian, PSCR is not a cure. At best, it might add a year or two of life. In the short time between recovering from her double mastectomy and the start of PSCR, I believed our spring garden could wait.

Following her morning devotions, Vivian would often suggest we plant.

"Honey," I would say, "you need your rest."

As the days slipped by, I hand-watered our plants on the windowsill. In fact, I was reluctant to plant a spring garden; I feared its harvest would be in jeopardy. Under the best of circumstances, which Vivian's were not, PSCR takes a month to finish; some patients are in the hospital for up to three months. With our focus on Vivian's survival, I wondered who would tend and weed the garden.

On the morning before the City of Hope began to harvest her blood for stem cells, Vivian was insistent. "Today is the day," she told me, smiling weakly. "We need to plant our garden together."

As the sun burned through a marine layer, I pulled the lounge chair from the back porch and placed it near the garden. I smiled at her, spaded the soil, and marveled at my wife's determination and will. Through her love and faith, she held on to the smallest thread of hope. We planted gardens together. Through her exhaustion, in the way she looked at me, I understood she could already picture its harvest.

Vivian planted one or two vegetables, and I insisted she rest. To the rhythm of my spade and the soil, we spoke of the beauty surrounding us. Vivian asked me if I remembered moving to our house on Foxglove Court in the winter of 1993.

There wasn't any landscaping, I recalled, unless dirt and rocks count.

We both remarked how quickly the grass had taken hold. The three oak trees we had planted were now throwing thick shade. The fruit trees, seeded around the garden, were ripening in surprising yields: pomegranates, lemons, tangerines, and oranges. We had cultivated, nourished, and cared for the three-tiered garden of our shared design and creation. Over the years, a rich soil base produced greater and greater harvests.

We noticed how the bougainvillea had grown to cover the screened-in area of our entire back porch. I told her I imagined some of the vines could be more than forty feet in length. In our spring garden, Vivian and I looked around with a combination of accomplishment and amazement. We had done this together.

Vivian, of course, was the one to first suggest the metaphor of harvest for our work together at Azusa Pacific University. We believed the tasks of gardening—seeding, nourishing, weeding, cultivating, and harvesting—came closest to describing our jobs in Christian higher education. As Vivian watched me plant in the soil, our conversation shifted to the upcoming graduation. We discussed names of students we believed capable of marking the world with the love of Christ. On a much deeper level—soul instead of soil—we shared a calling in Kingdom work. In a very real sense, gardening was our shared mission.

I reminded Vivian once again that she had been the one to hear the small whisper of God to come to Azusa Pacific University. In 1990, renewed in a commitment to each other and our calling, we worked as a leadership team to develop the necessary physical, human, and spiritual resources for a productive harvest.

On that spring morning eight years later, we reminded each other how God had blessed. Programs had blossomed. Enrollment had doubled, and, in some cases, tripled and quadrupled. A west campus had been started, and eight new buildings had sprung up from the dirt. While I planted, we smiled when we looked at one another. Without speaking, we understood our work together as a source of deep joy.

In our spring garden, Vivian and I looked at each other with a combination of accomplishment and amazement.

Through God's grace and power, we had accomplished much together.

In our lives, we shared a harvest of eternal significance.

I planted the last of our spring garden in a lingering silence, falling into a rhythm of digging. When I finished, I reached over and extended my hand to my wife and partner. When I pulled her to her feet, she held me in her arms.

"I'm sorry," she whispered in my ear, "that things will never be the same."

❖ ❖ ❖

On the first Monday following the planting of our spring garden, Vivian began stem cell apheresis. Rooted in the Greek word meaning "to separate," apheresis is the process of breaking down blood into its various components—platelets, white blood cells, red blood cells, and stem cells. The purpose of apheresis is to harvest a sufficient number of peripheral blood stem cells so that, following high-dose chemotherapy, they might resurrect a patient's damaged and suppressed bone marrow. The harvest of these mother or seed cells is collected in plastic bags, tested, frozen, and refrigerated until Day Zero. After the patient has received a nearly lethal bombardment of chemical toxins, the peripheral blood stem cells are infused back into the bloodstream where they do their mysterious work.

For four hours a day for the next seven days, Vivian's blood circulated through a machine, which through the process of centrifugal force separated it into its various elements. On one of the first days of Vivian's apheresis, I remember her watching the various layers appear before us. "When you have a terminal illness," she told me, "your life is like that—it separates into layers."

You harvest only what is of lasting value.

113

16   IT IS WELL
WITH MY SOUL

PSCR is based on a simple idea: If you are losing a war, order more powerful artillery. Instead of a few carefully lobbed grenades, unleash an atomic bomb. Do whatever it takes to kill the cancer before it kills you. The fallout of high- dose chemotherapy is great. To her normal description of chemotherapy—"the cure that kills"—Vivian added "absolutely."

The Hickman catheter is a long tube inserted into a major vein leading directly to the right atrium of the heart. Throughout PSCR, the catheter is used to administer medicines, intravenous fluids, and cytotoxic drugs. Through her Hickman catheter, which Vivian had had inserted into her leg instead of her badly damaged chest, she received seven days of high-dose chemotherapy, which in Vivian's case included the highly toxic chemicals carboplatin, Taxol, and cyclosporin. In administering the poison cocktail, great care is taken to avoid any leakage. Just a drop eats through the skin.

> *In a few hours I will begin the ordeal of being saturated with toxic chemicals. I am here in the Village at the City of Hope with [my closest girlfriend] Carol Wagstaff. Already this morning I have taken my last shower for four days, had the nurse come to do my blood draw, taken all my meds, and eaten breakfast. Father, you have brought me to this point. I am still alive.*

116

While Vivian received her first high dose of chemotherapy—a bright green fluid flowing through her catheter—Carol sang to her. In a shared history dating back to their college days, the singing was one of several running jokes the two shared. As Vivian reclined in a hospital bed at the City of Hope, Carol sang a verse of "It Is Well with My Soul," one of their favorites.

> *When peace like a river attendeth my way,*
> *When sorrows like sea-billows roll;*
> *Whatever my lot, Thou hast taught me to say,*
> *"It is well, it is well with my soul."*

Then without pause or transition, she slipped into the theme song for *The Brady Bunch.* Even during her first treatment of high-dose chemotherapy, Vivian found that Carol could still be counted on for a good laugh. The two women felt at ease with each other—they could step outside expectations and titles and remain unguarded. They extended to one another the listening and forgiving ear of a high priest. Just as important, they could encourage each other to laugh and dream.

Together, as the poison dripped into Vivian's bloodstream, they recalled times together long ago and a half a country away. Vivian and Carol spoke of spring mornings on campus, football games on fall afternoons, old flames, and the color a future looks when seen through the eyes of youth.

When the nurse interrupted to adjust Vivian's IV, Carol tried not to notice her friend wince. Over time, they learned to prefer laughter over tears. After Carol once heard Vivian talk about the grandchildren she might never see, there was an awkward silence and a welling up of tears. Picking up another of their running jokes, Carol, whose family had a history of Alzheimer's, said she would die brainless before Vivian died breastless. And then who would sing her songs?

117

✦ ✦ ✦

During these seven days of high-dose chemotherapy, Vivian was living at the Village at the City of Hope. A series of duplex apartments on beautifully landscaped grounds, one of the Village's unstated purposes is to protect others from the screams.

Before our first day in the Village, seven family members and friends gathered at the City of Hope to receive instructions. For the next few weeks, we were to rotate in round-the-clock shifts and share in Vivian's care. We learned how to dispense medications and painkillers, care for the Hickman catheter, monitor vital statistics, and clean, cook, and live according to strict regulations. Only canned food, we learned, was permitted—otherwise Vivian faced a greater risk from bacteria. No fingernail clippers were allowed—because of destroyed platelets, a tiny cut could be fatal. Live plant arrangements were forbidden due to the deadly potential of mold.

We were shown how to page the nurse to come immediately. We were warned about the intensity of hallucinations—an occasional side effect of the drug dexamethasone given during and after Day Zero to prevent allergic reactions such as fatal brain swelling.

Looking back on the twenty-eight days we spent in the Village, I have only disconnected memories—vivid and fragmented images. As a microcosm of the suffering Vivian endured in her war with the Beast, only intensified, I often recall these events with the detached observations of a spectator. In the surreal melding of horror and boredom, time seemed to unfold before us like the clumsy frames of old black-and-white movies. I could never shake the feeling that little seemed to flow logically or continuously.

I remember one bright morning when Vivian and I were transported in a plastic-domed golf cart across to the hospital. Moving through the grounds of the Village, we noticed the waving banners and shouts of encouragement that often came from the parking lots of the duplexes.

| WE LOVE YOU, BRIAN |

| KEEP FIGHTING, BRIAN |

| YOU ARE OUR HERO |

From RVs and pickup trucks, family and friends were cheering a patient in a golf cart riding slightly in front of us. While Vivian and I watched as we followed a curve in the road, we saw an eight-year-old boy looking out over the cheering supporters. His head was tilted in a half-embarrassed, fully proud manner. Like Vivian, he wanted to believe his life was not nearly over.

I remember the afternoons and evenings, with Vivian rising occasionally from stupor and pain to make certain we were having fun; I remember the endless string of board games, reassuring words, and smells from canned foods.

I remember the first night after Day Zero. In the low pastel glow of the intravenous pump, Vivian bolted upright in bed like a rake when you step on its teeth. Her eyes were wide and full of panic. "Get them off me!" she screamed. I took her hand and noticed she was clammy, sweating. She looked into my eyes and pleaded. "Get them off me!" When she screamed again, I understood where the term *bloodcurdling* came from. She began to writhe on the sheets. Fearing she would rip herself from monitors and intravenous medicine, I tried to hold her still. I pressed the button for the nurse.

"Richard!" Vivian yelled again. "Get these insects off of me! Get them off; they are eating me alive!" I remember when the nurse arrived, she reassured me it was just a hallucination. The best I could do was speak gently to my wife and hold her hand.

119

✦ ✦ ✦

During PSCR, engraftment occurs when the body's immune system, measured in blood counts, has shown itself capable of reproduction. Once the number of platelets and white and red blood cells reach certain levels—usually ten to fourteen days after Day Zero—the patient is soon free to return home.

On one of the nights she anxiously awaited her mother's engraftment, Melissa decided to read aloud. She had brought a copy of one of the Chicken Soup books to the Village in an assured hope of generating at least a mild case of warm fuzzy feelings. Although her mother was no longer hallucinating, she would often awake and, knotted in a foreboding depression, fail to get back to sleep. When she did so again that night, Melissa opened her book and read the first story she came upon.

As it slowly revealed itself, the story centered around a mother who was dying of cancer. Because she understood she did not have much longer to live, the pages spoke of the various videotapes she prepared to give to her daughter. On each label, she specified the date on which her daughter should watch the video—on her sixteenth birthday, at graduation, on her wedding day, etc.

Although both Vivian and Melissa were slowly horrified at the inappropriate timing of the story, Melissa continued to read. What else could she do—stop reading and acknowledge the despair? On her deathbed, the mother in the story made a terrible realization. She had not recorded the most important tape. Onto a blank cassette, a nurse wrote and pasted a final label: *Watch on your father's wedding day.* Then into a camera, the woman spoke her dying words: "Be nice to your new mother."

When Melissa finished the story, she remembers a terrible silence broken only by rhythmic clicks and whirs of the machines and monitors that surrounded them.

✦ ✦ ✦

In the wake of PSCR, I wrestled with what amount of suffering we would trade for the dimming hope of cure. If I had known then what I know now, I would have quit my job in January 1998, and Vivian and I would have traveled the world as we had always planned. In the end, we left final decisions about treatment to Vivian. She always held out for the possibility—no matter how slim—of extending her life. In the terror of impending death, Vivian learned to appreciate the incalculable value of each everyday moment.

Two weeks after PSCR, Vivian and I left for a ten-day vacation in the Rocky Mountains with Melissa and our son-in-law, Lance. Everyone shared the deepest hope that Vivian's recent ordeal would provide dividends of a longer life, even if it was just a year or two, as the most optimistic statistics indicated.

We were all amazed with Vivian's awareness and energy. While sitting on the backseat of a tandem powered mostly by Lance, we rode with a picnic to the waterfalls. We laughed and Vivian pointed out the beauty.

As she read devotions from Oswald Chambers, Vivian paused to ask us to listen to a thunderstorm high in the mountains and notice how its echoes fell down glacial peaks.

Vivian made her famous French dip sandwiches, and while we were eating, we spotted a blue heron flying.

Where the Continental Divide opens at Berthoud Pass and the raging Colorado River finds its headwaters, we rented a pontoon boat and crossed Grand Lake to Shadow Mountain.

Under a chilling mist of rain, Vivian and Melissa, each giggling, wrapped up in a parka together.

On the Fourth of July, we sat on a balcony overlooking the lake and watched the fireworks thread pastel colors on still and pristine waters.

When Vivian was exhausted by a hike down Adams Falls Trail, we all napped near a waterfall.

Following a vacation Melissa described as her best ever, we told her and Lance good-bye.

THE GRACE OF
TRANSFORMATION

17 HUMAN WEAKNESS, DIVINE POWER

July 23, 1998
Lord Jesus, you know my deepest fears—you know
that I think the cancer has come back and is now
growing in my skin, my liver, and my brain. This
is my death sentence and yet, Lord, there is hope.

To the doctors at the City of Hope she was responsible for teaching, Dr. Lucille Leong would point out that in addition to the patients who make life stressful, they should be prepared to wrestle with maintaining a professional attitude in caring for a woman like Vivian. That, she said, would be a true test of their ability to endure.

In nearly every sense, Vivian was for Lucille a quintessential case study in the medical category of "difficult." It was difficult for Lucille, for example, to lock eyes on Vivian for the first time and see someone so much like herself—professional, intelligent, Asian-American, of the same sex, and nearly the same age. It was difficult for her, over time, to watch someone so lovely, so full of grace, and with so much to live for lose so much—her beauty, her hair, her skills, her speech, her coordination, and finally her life. It was difficult for her, time after time, to report only bad news to someone so focused on hope, cooperation, and perseverance. It was difficult to have to tell someone with so much faith that the storybook ending had been rewritten.

126

On July 27, 1998—just a little more than six weeks after Vivian endured high-dose chemotherapy with peripheral stem cell rescue—Dr. Leong was faced with telling her that the biopsy of a small lump was positive for cancer and that malignant lesions had been discovered in her lungs. In an effort to brace herself for the meeting, Dr. Leong called on her spiritual resources. As she had many times previously, she prayed: *Lord, help me. Help me to do this right.*

July 30, 1998

This recurrence on the chest wall means I am at stage IV— there is no cure for me—the cancer is winning the battle. In fact, it has speeded up its growth and aggressiveness. I can almost see it growing day to day. It is terrifying to think of the cancer growing rapidly through my body.

I am trusting you, Lord. I trust your goodness and your grace. I claim your promise to hear and answer prayer. You have kept me and blessed me—even when I didn't want you, even when I denied you—you kept pouring blessings on

me. Now I am in a blind alley—there are no doors or
windows here—only your grace and power.
*   I have nothing to offer, nothing to give. I am empty and*
without hope that life can continue—except for your mercy.

For the next several months, Vivian endured a series of alternative treatments, which included an experimental drug, a Mexican clinic offering a combination of diet and meditation, electrochemical therapy, and Chinese herbs. At the start of each new regimen, Vivian would always pray for the best.

Who knows? Maybe this is the miracle we have been
looking for.

On her drive down to the clinic in Tijuana, Carol Wagstaff looked forward to spending the weekend with her old friend. Since first hearing from Vivian about the Gerson Clinic, which offered alternative treatments combining diet and meditation to build a patient's immune system, Carol had circled the weekend of August 23–24 on her calendar.

During a tour of the clinic, Carol learned of the demanding and intricate regimen of a mostly juice diet, reflexology, and meditation. After hearing of treatments involving vitamins, liver extracts, ion exchange, and ozone therapy, Carol found the fodder for her next running joke: Vivian's daily schedule of five coffee enemas. From then on, the times they spent with one another would include at least one reference: "Time for a coffee, anyone?"

Carol was not ready to relinquish hope for her old friend. Despite the dire warnings of the traditional medical community about

Vivian's inevitable slide into death, Carol believed her friend would be miraculously healed. After listening attentively to the clinic's philosophy and treatment, Carol gave Vivian a gift: a book called *Christ the Healer*. Drawn together by a long history of looking forward to the future, these two friends viewed Vivian's cancer as incongruous with their plans. There had to be some deeper reason for it. Having experienced the pain of adversity in her own life, Carol believed Vivian would likewise be pruned by the hand of God. Having suffered and finally been healed, Vivian would produce greater harvests in whatever ministry God would reveal to her.

Vivian, Carol noticed, seemed unsure of her own healing. She spoke less than usual and more in the present tense. Although she still prayed for and sought a miracle, Vivian was more settled than desperate. Carol wrestled for the first time with her previously unflappable belief that Vivian would be healed. As they ended a time of worship together, Carol quoted Isaiah 57:1, which had been recently troubling her: "The righteous perish, and no one ponders it in his heart; devout men are taken away, and no one understands."

Carol had to confess to Vivian: She was more than a little confused as to why God had not yet acted on Vivian's behalf. For the longest time, Vivian did not respond. Tilting her head back slightly to feel the warm rays of sun streaming in through the window, she seemed to be peacefully turning over a Scripture in her mind, holding it this way and that, as if the meaning depended upon finding just the right perspective.

"What is man that you are mindful of him," Vivian quoted from a psalm, "the son of man that you care for him? You made him a little lower than the angels; you crowned him with glory and honor, and put everything under his feet."

Once again, Vivian paused. She closed her eyes, and her lips moved silently. Just as Carol was about to renew her complaint with God, Vivian resumed reciting Scripture from memory, quoting from Hebrews 2: "In putting everything under him, God left nothing that is not subject to him. Yet at present we do not see everything subject to him. But we see Jesus, who was made a little lower than the angels, now crowned with glory and honor because he suffered death, so that by the grace of God he might taste death for everyone."

Late that summer Vivian wrote in her journal:

129

Amazingly, with each recurrence my faith has grown stronger. In one way, the worse my prognosis becomes, the greater the opportunities for God's power to be displayed. At least more of my hope and faith have been placed in him as the best of medical science has failed me.

There truly is no treatment left for me. All I have is faith in the goodness of God.

Yesterday when Richard and I were doing our devotions, I looked out and there was a beautiful yellow and black butterfly trapped against the sunscreen covering the patio roof. When insects fly onto the porch, they fly up to escape and become trapped by the screen. If only the butterfly would have flown down, it could have easily flown away, but it struggled and struggled against the screen. Like the others, it would have died of exhaustion or a blackbird would have caught and eaten it.

I stopped Richard's reading and told him about the butterfly. He immediately went out, got the pool net, and tried to maneuver the butterfly by lifting the screen so it could fly out. The butterfly kept trying to escape into the corner so that Richard couldn't get it with his net. He tried for many minutes, several times banging and crunching the butterfly. Finally, from exhaustion, the butterfly landed on the net. Richard took the net into the yard and held it until the butterfly realized it could just fly away.

Only by trusting in the Lord could Vivian rest in her struggle against the illness. A couple of weeks after returning from Mexico, Vivian was thrilled to hear from Dr. Leong that she had won the "compassion lottery." Each month, a national drawing was conducted to determine who would be treated with the latest experimental drug.

130

Herceptin is one of the new class of gene therapy drugs. Its purpose is to block the gene which makes my cancer so aggressive. It has not been approved yet by the FDA and is still available only to terminal women who are positive for HER2/neu. The early reports on the effectiveness of Herceptin have been encouraging.

The next step is now to schedule all the baseline tests—blood work, mega scan, CAT scan, bone scan, chest X-rays, EKG. These will help monitor the effectiveness of Herceptin. We are thanking the Lord for this unexpected blessing and are praising him for sending help just when the skin metastases are getting really ugly and painful.

Our joy was short-lived. Two months after beginning to take the drug, Vivian learned that the Herceptin had failed to slow the assault of the Beast.

Against the backdrop of failing medical treatments, each one's results less hopeful than the one before, Vivian learned a great lesson about life. Quoting Mother Teresa, she wrote in a journal:

We cannot do great things on this earth—we can only do little things with great love!

In an e-mail to friends and colleagues, Vivian expressed her gratitude for the love she had learned:

✉ Throughout these years of continuous treatment, I feel as if everything has been stripped away from me—physically and emotionally—by the surgeon's scalpel, radiation, and toxic chemicals. But I can tell you his grace is sufficient and nothing compares to the joy of knowing Christ. God has dealt bountifully with me and been ever gracious. My only regret is for much of my life I was not aware of this. Thank you for all of your prayers and acts of friendship. These have been a great part of his bounty toward me.

131

Who knows? Maybe those *were* the miracles we were looking for.

18
THE
DYING SEED

As Vivian sought to make rhyme or reason of her suffering, she came to a new appreciation for the power of metaphor. She quoted Malcolm Muggeridge in the margins of a journal:

> *Every happening is a parable from God.*
> *The art of life is in figuring what it means.*

The critical issues of life, she believed, could not be understood by the linear and often one-dimensional movement of logic; rather, deeper meaning found its blossom in the intuitions of art. In her frequent prayers to God for "new eyes to see," she instinctively and increasingly understood that vision to be symbolic.

Already grounded in the rich history of literature, Vivian was graced by God with various languages of metaphor—dream, vision, intuition, and image—starting with her dream, months before her diagnosis, of a tumor that sprang from her heart, grew, festered, and fell into the soil—the seed of a radiant flower's blossom. As she battled in the wasteland of cancer—what she called her Gethsemane experience—again and again she experienced the imagery of the garden. In the dream of the basement garden room, she watched impossibly white and soft light falling like water into an underground room filled with ripe fruits and vegetables. From the life of Teresa of Avila, a sixteenth-century desert mother, she took notes comparing the maturity of prayer to the watering of a garden: well and bucket, winch and winnows, irrigation and torrential rain.

Into a prepared and tended garden, a seed falls. Out of death comes life. From the festering tumor, a greening plant rises and blooms. From a basement room, a garden impossibly grows. In the desert, a flower opens. In the metaphors and images of Vivian's dreams and experiences, the central theme was the same: life impossibly rising from death.

In mid-November, just days before Dr. Leong told Vivian she could expect four to six weeks more of life, Vivian had a vision and a dream on the same day. In an afternoon vision, she saw a woman standing in a falling and flowing stream of pooling white light. When the woman stepped from the light and shed a layer of diseased skin, Vivian recognized her own face. Feeling pure, clean, and renewed, she experienced the sensation of weightlessness—an emptying—and the gratitude of one healed.

In the afternoon I had the sense (and a vision) of myself shedding my heavy diseased body like a coat and walking

away from it. But I understood that this was more in a spiri-
tual sense rather than a physical sense.

On the night following the vision of shedding her disease, Vivian had a dream that she equated with a seeding of faith.

I dreamed that the Holy Spirit came to me and filled me.
I could feel my head being touched by him and his presence
being poured into me.

Until the end, Vivian did not quite know what to make of her visions and dreams. She wrestled with their ambiguity and harbored suspicions about their credibility; at the same time, she could never deny the power of the symbols: soil, seed, light, and fruit. In each of her dreams or visions, she was reminded of Scripture.

135

Listen carefully: Unless a grain of wheat is buried in the ground, dead to the world, it is never any more than a grain of wheat. But if it is buried, it sprouts and reproduces itself many times over. In the same way, any one who holds on to life just as it is destroys that life. But if you let it go, reckless in your love, you'll have it forever.
(John 12: 24-25, *The Message*)

19 PARTING WORDS

We have now entered the realm of faith—how do I believe for healing and how do I prepare for death, without one hurting or damaging the other? But no matter what happens I know that you will be with me and will keep me in your care.

Following the news she could expect four to six weeks to live, Vivian chose her direction at our fork in the road: She would prepare to die, while I shouldered the responsibility of praying for her healing. She enrolled in the school of dying graces knowing full well that its tuition would cost her nothing less than everything.

Thank you. I yield my life and my future to you. I give you all that I can give you at

*this moment—my faith, my hope, my desires for healing,
and my life. It is in your hands. I yield to your wisdom
and plan. Blessed be the Lord, who daily loads us
with benefits, the God of our salvation! Our God is the
God of salvation; and from God alone comes escape from
death.*

One of the most difficult lessons for Vivian was learning to say good-bye to friends and family. After dying in so many slow pieces, she had already lost so much—her breasts, her comfort, her independence, her physical skills, and much of her hope for the future.

It is not the dying that is hard, but the leaving.

As we entered into the holiday season of 1998, Vivian knew it would be her last. With her family and greater community, she took seriously the lessons in saying good-bye.

✦ ✦ ✦

On December 6, 1998, six hundred people from Azusa Pacific University came to visit Vivian at our open house. Vivian sat on our back porch, wrapped in a blanket, propped by pillows, briefly greeting each person with a smile.

The next day, Vivian wrote:

*At this point, it appears there will be no physical healing. All
of this again has been devastating for us. My first reaction is,
"God, why don't you hear the prayers of your people?" I don't
understand. But I know he has been here with me every*

minute. We know the future looks very bleak. It is heart-breaking for me to know what I am putting my family through. We know that God can still step in and do a miracle for us, but we are busy planning for the end. It is not easy. We had hoped there would be some time to do some fun things as a family, but we will have to wait and see.

On the day after Christmas, Vivian suggested we pack a picnic and head off for the Indian Canyons near Palm Springs. On a lovely winter's morning, our family—Doak, his girlfriend, Stephanie, Tris, Melissa, Lance, Vivian, and I rode through a desert to an oasis. As Vivian unpacked leftovers from Christmas dinner, the family hiked over rocks shaded by palm trees growing lush by springs of water and gentle streams. Bordered by the Tahquitz, Palm, and Andreas Canyons, the oasis was once known by the Cahuilla Indians as Se-Khi—"boiling water"—and renamed by the Spanish as Aqua Caliente—hot water. In its green contrast to surrounding desert, the effect of the land's beauty is startling. Although Vivian was too weak to walk great distances, she insisted we explore. She was content to listen to the sound of water, distant voices, and laughter. During her ordeal with cancer, the love of family for Vivian was like a stream running through parched and barren land.

In the hours spent in the beauty of the desert oasis, Vivian laughed along with the rest of us. She was experiencing the overwhelming beauty and grace pregnant in each passing moment— the sound of palm leaves in the wind; the color of her children's eyes in a low sun; the view from high ground; the subtle taste of watermelon. As a family, we had a wonderful time. Only once did we have cause for concern. On a short hike, Vivian fell on some rocks, cutting her hands and legs. As we helped her to her feet, she apologized. She expressed some concern that she was spoiling everyone's joy.

The following evening, nestled once again as a family in our place by the ocean, Tris was less than enthusiastic with his mom's idea of taking a walk on the beach. With the sun setting, he understood a chill would settle into the air—at least by Californian standards. He had to be prodded to move out of his easy chair, which his mother was only too happy to do. As usual, Vivian won over the family with her strength of conviction about the perfect activity.

After the whole family walked together for a few minutes, Tris and his mother seemed to lag behind the rest of us. Side by side, hand in hand, speaking to one another of the beauty, they walked through tide pools softly reflecting the colors of silver and indigo. As darkness crept along the eastern skies, following them like a half-understood whisper, they stopped along a scattering of rocks at the beach's end to watch the sun disappear. In the wake of a horizon filled with the blazing and impossible hues of purple, red, and pink fading to grays and blues, Tris's mother spoke to him of her delight in a sunset. At no other point in time did she so feel the presence of God. As the full sun touched the horizon, she whispered to Tris her desire to stand up and walk into its light—into the arms of God. With one arm wrapped around his mother's shoulder, Tris held her and they wept together.

Once the family caught up with the two of them, Tris decided to remain behind. While he prayed, a dull reflection from the rising moon came from the sand. Picking up a small rock—smooth, pear-shaped, and deep black—Tris was intrigued by its appearance. As a memento of his last walk on the beach with his mother, he slipped it into his pocket.

✦ ✦ ✦

On the morning of December 28—a day before she was to return with her husband to Colorado—Melissa wondered what her mother was typing on the computer. After having requested a family meeting, Vivian had been unable to speak what was on her mind; she asked for our patience as she wrote a letter. For twenty minutes or so, Melissa stood with the rest of us, nervously sipping a beverage, wondering what her mother had in mind. After printing several copies, Vivian handed each of us the letter. She requested that we read it individually and then discuss it afterward.

It didn't take long for Melissa to figure out the letter was saying good-bye.

> Dec. 28, 1998
> Dear loved ones,
> It is very hard for me to talk about death, so I am writing this. When I think about leaving you all, I cannot do so without a great sorrow and a multitude of tears. My heart is very full as I write this.
> This year is going to be a very difficult one for all of you, especially your dad. It will probably include a continued decline of my energy and abilities and functioning. I know that Dr. Leong will try at least two or three types of chemotherapy and each may add a few good months, but it is likely that crisis times will come followed by a brief respite until one day she

will say, "Call hospice." Then you will know there are two or three weeks left.

I am very fortunate to have so much love and support from all of you, and from friends both near and far. I am also grateful I have the opportunity to tell you these things now. There will be plenty of time to say good-bye. As you know, this is the thing that haunted me so when my father died—I didn't get to say good-bye. You will each have a big hole in your lives for a while and then a little one always. Your dad will have the biggest empty place and feel very lost for a long time; be sure and comfort him.

I want your father to get married again; he will need the love and companionship. I hope you will love and accept whoever it is. I know that it will change family dynamics in relationships, but you can all adjust and create new family.

Later, I will write to each of you kids and tell you individual things, but for now let me say that I do have a few regrets about life. I regret that I didn't realize sooner how very precious life is and how much I should have savored each moment instead of always wanting more. I regret that there isn't time to do so many of the things I wanted to do, but I have already done more than I ever dreamed in my life, and I am so very grateful. My greatest regret is that I will never be able to love and help raise my grandchildren. I wanted to pray for them every day of their lives, just as each of you has been prayed for. But I know that God will provide someone to make up for this in their lives. Please tell them about me, and how much I love them even now unborn.

My words are to you: Embrace life, go after your dreams, but learn that each moment with loved ones is the most wonderful thing life has to offer. It is the small pleasures that bring the most satisfaction—a bite of Chunky Monkey, puppy slippers, scratching a dog, smelling a baby's skin, lots of laughter, cuddling with the ones you love—so imprint those on your memory so that they will sustain you in later years.

I hope that you will give these things priority in life:

1. **God.** Talk to him daily and learn to know him intimately. You will find that he is infinitely good and gracious. I am confident he will keep watch over you and never leave you alone. Find a church that will be a supportive community to you and your children.

2. **Your families.** Make meals and prayer times together a priority. Teach discipline and obedience. Have lots of fun.

3. **Work.** Work is noble and the offering we give to God and our families. It is how we define ourselves and feel satisfaction in what we create. You will find the neater and more organized you are, the happier you will be.

4. **Friends.** You have all been blessed with lots of friends; you will continue to make new ones and recycle the old ones—don't lose the good ones.

I'm going to spend the next few months giving away some of the things which are precious to me; very few will have great value, but I hope you will value the things I designate for you.

You have been and are wonderful kids. The Lord has blessed each of you with physical bodies that are beautiful and function well. You are each so good-looking, which has made us proud, and you have good minds and learn quickly. Best of all you have a loving and compassionate nature, which makes *me the proudest; you care about others and know how to show it. Don't take any of these gifts for granted. Take care of your minds, bodies, and spirits, value all your qualities, and continue to work on your weaknesses.*

My greatest desire is to welcome each of you into heaven, just as I know my father will be waiting for me. Please live so that this will be so, and remember it is the grace of God and your belief in Jesus Christ that will be the final determiner of your eternal dwelling place.

Our true selves are kind of like a big house with lots of rooms. As you go through life, explore all the rooms and keep them well tended. The room I have not wanted to visit is labeled "death," but I have a suspicion that rather than being a dark, horror-filled room, it is a cozy place with an easy chair and a fireplace. But big enough for only one. Someday—maybe this year—I will visit that room and find death as a friend who will release me from pain. I will simply cross that threshold and step into the arms of Jesus.

Many times we have sat at the beach watching the sunset and I thought how wonderful it would simply be to step into the sunset and into the world where God himself will wipe away every tear. So when you see me in every sunset remember I am waiting just on the other side; I long for the great reunion when we will all be together again. I love you more than I can say.

After reading the letter, Melissa could not talk without weeping. When she cried, her mother also could not hold back her tears. Instead of saying words, Melissa held her mother in her arms for the longest time.

✦ ✦ ✦

During a New Year's Eve party planned and prepared by his mother, our oldest son, Doak, announced his engagement to Stephanie. Doak understood more than anyone how pleased his mother was about his wedding date: April 10, 1999. With an expected life span nearly exhausted, he knew it gave her a strong motivation to keep fighting and living.

20 IMAGES OF HEAVEN

Just before a weeklong trip to Hawaii in February 1999, we sold our place by the ocean. Even though recent tests reported the cancer's growth had slowed, Vivian understood she would die. When asked if I would use the condominium after her death, I said I could not live in a home in which we had planned to retire together. With great sorrow, we decided to sell. On January 30, 1999, as we walked through our place at Dana Point for the last time, we both understood it as a sign of the end. After thanking God for so many wonderful times, we walked away from a part of our past and any specific hope for a future.

After I locked the door, Vivian cried and cried.

On our only previous trip to Hawaii—in 1996, before the cancer—Vivian had fallen in love with the lonely, almost mystical beauty of Kauai, the oldest and smallest of the four major islands. She recalled the plane ride we had taken near the Na Pali Coast, where volcanic mountains rise steeply from the ocean's floor. Moving through rising mists and lush green trees, the pilot had pointed out Mount Wai'ale'ale, the island's volcanic birthplace.

Now, on our return trip, Vivian was the one to suggest a helicopter flight into the volcano.

We understood the vacation in Hawaii to be our swan song. As her cancer loosened its death grip slightly, we spent seven days in what is often considered this planet's most perfect image of paradise. After days filled with slow walks, holding hands on the beach, and remembering our life together, we decided to fly into the mythical Mount Wai'ale'ale. According to science, this was the first mountain to rise above the ocean and, through a gradual flow of lava, form the island of Kauai. As ancient legend had it, the priests of a polytheistic religion lived in volcanic craters offering sacrifices to a dangerous and powerful creative beauty.

When Vivian suggested the helicopter ride, she asked me, "Wouldn't it be wonderful to go to a place only the intermediaries of gods could go?"

✦ ✦ ✦

Rain is responsible for Kauai's breathtaking beauty. Known as "the garden island," its jungles are clogged with unstoppable growth. Clouds blown inland from the ocean move, gather, and cool. And it rains and rains on Mount Wai'ale'ale—one of the most wet and fertile spots on the planet. From the creases of volcanic mountains, etched by fingers of lava, the water runs, cascading down thousands of waterfalls, the capillaries of thick and green jungles wild with fecundity.

As we passed over Manaowaipuna Falls, dropping three hundred feet, we spoke of heaven for the first time together. *Will the mist still feel wet? Will the valleys be as green and narrow as these?* As we flew into the Waimea Canyon, which a thunderstruck Mark Twain named the Grand Canyon of the Pacific, we asked one another: *At any point will heaven dive three thousand feet into ground? Will you be able to sift the soil between your fingers, and will such greening life spring from it?* Over cliffs green and purple and blue and red, we saw rainbows in misty skies. *In heaven, will we see colors the same, changing in various movements of light? Can there be any places more lovely than these, painted in hues so radiant with rain?*

149

Rounding the bay along the Na Pali Coast, where Vivian had first been inspired to one day fly into the volcàno, we were speechless to see the rising of Mount Wai'ale'ale shrouded at its mouth with the sad and lovely clouds found in winter dreams. *Will heaven rise into the clouds, and will we be able to touch them, velvety like silver inside of dreams?*

Long after a cataclysmic eruption collapsed the northern wall of Mount Wai'ale'ale, estimated to have occurred 5.1 million years earlier, our helicopter flew through the open side into the heart of the ancient volcano, the genesis of such paradise and mystery, where only the priests had been rumored to live. *In heaven, will the face of God be fully unveiled?* For what seemed like the longest time, we hovered, the clouds above us. Only slowly did we begin to rise, holding hands as we climbed toward the shroud where the volcano's cone was hidden.

As we slowly rose, clouds and mists covered us like slow and ancient secrets. For what seemed like the longest time, we could see only a thick gray . . . rising, rising. The pilot was silent, and we trusted him. *In heaven will there be thick fogs and mysteries slowly revealed?* In a moment, near the mouth of the ancient volcano, we spilled into a blue, blue sky. *Dare we imagine,* Vivian asked me then, *what it will be like to see each other in heaven?*

21 GREAT LOSS, GREATER JOY

Upon our return from Hawaii in March, the Beast closed in for the kill. In a letter sent to the APU campus community, Vivian outlined a terrible meeting with Dr. Leong.

> *You have been on a long journey with us.*
> *Your love has filled it with hope and comfort. But now it has become more tortuous and difficult.*
>
> *The cancer has come back with a vengeance. My skin erupted and numerous new lesions appeared in the lungs. My doctor started me on Xeloda, which is an oral chemotherapy taken daily, but later I was having dizzy spells and problems with balance, writing, and thinking. My normal quick wit and memory were about five*

seconds off. Richard canceled a trip and took me to the hospital.

After asking me questions such as my name, date, and address and checking my eyes, muscle tone, balance, and handwriting, Dr. Leong immediately scheduled a brain MRI. The scans showed severe swelling of the brain as the result of a dozen or more brain tumors.

The treatment is whole brain radiation daily for ten days, and Decadron to reduce the swelling. This comes as the greatest blow to me as I am losing my ability to function normally. As you know, we have a wedding coming up next month, which should be a most joyful time for our family.

We covet your prayers as always. The Lord is very close and holding us tight in his arms.

After her oncologist told Vivian she had twelve brain tumors, some as large as quarters, Vivian gave Dr. Leong a present—a book entitled *Intimate Moments with the Savior* by Ken Gire. Once again, Vivian was proving to be a very difficult patient. When others might have reacted with rage or depression, Vivian was giving of herself.

After hearing the terrible news, Vivian's most pressing concern was her oldest son's wedding on April 10. Vivian not only planned on attending the nuptials, but she also wanted to walk down the aisle. God willing, she would take the celebrated seat as the proud mother of the groom. Although Dr. Leong promised she would do everything she could, once again the doctor had to call up spiritual reserves to believe in the medical possibility. The cancer was growing rapidly in Vivian's brain, pressing into critical areas of speech, cognition, and coordination. With some good fortune, Vivian might be alive for the wedding, but walking down the aisle would require a good deal of faith.

◆ ◆ ◆

From my crouching position in our spring garden, I looked up and smiled at my wife. Over my strong objections, on a sunny Southern Californian morning just before Easter, Vivian insisted I plant. It would do her good, she said, to see me working my hands in the dirt. Lying in her blue lounge chair, covered by a blue afghan, she had fallen asleep while watching.

On the second tier of our three-tiered garden, in the shade of pomegranates and oaks we had planted years before, I was struck again with Vivian's loveliness. Past her wasted body and a face swollen and pocked by radiation to her brain, I couldn't help but see only her beauty. A few verses of Scripture from 2 Corinthians 4 leaped to my mind.

> Therefore we do not lose heart. Though outwardly we are wasting away, yet inwardly we are being renewed day by day. For our light and momentary troubles are achieving for us an eternal glory that far outweighs them all. (vv. 16-17)

I remembered back to the first time I saw her—her hair backlit in the passenger seat of a blue convertible: MY, MY, MY, MY, MY! I shook my head in acknowledgment. After thirty-four years of marriage, I understood this was our last spring garden. As she slept peacefully, I realized I had no hope for its harvest.

Three days before Easter Sunday, Carol Wagstaff came to see Vivian, who could not get out of bed. Instead of their traditional greeting—a firm and loving hug—Carol chose to lean over and rub her cheek softly against Vivian's; she could see her friend was in terrible pain. As she gingerly sat down on the comforter, Carol feared that Doak's mother might not be there for his wedding, which was less than two weeks away. Vivian struggled to talk, even breathe. Because of a necrotic, electrochemically treated tumor on her left side, she could only lie on one side. The steroids used to reduce the swelling of her tumors during brain radiation had rendered her muscles nearly useless.

Vivian smiled up at her old friend and asked, "Are you coming to Doak's wedding to see me walk down the aisle?"

Carol said she wouldn't miss it for the world.

As the evening light faded through the windows of the bedroom, Carol handed Vivian some of her homemade chicken soup, which had become as much of a tradition as a song of introduction. For her listening pleasure, Carol said "The Senility Prayer."

> *God grant me the senility*
> *To forget the people*
> *I never liked anyway,*
> *The good fortune*
> *To run into the ones I do,*
> *And the eyesight*
> *To tell the difference.*

In Vivian's fragile laughter was this acknowledgment: Carol could always make her laugh. As they began to reminisce about the old times, Carol continued another tradition: the giving of a foot massage.

"Do you remember us both directing that play while we were teaching high school?" Vivian asked. To keep the joke running, Carol responded she could not remember much of anything anymore.

"And who was that football player you went out with?" Vivian slowly asked. "And what was up with him, anyway?"

Propped by pillows, having allowed time for her breath to return, Vivian took a sip or two. She loved her old friend's soup.

"Do you remember what we used to eat when we were pregnant together with our first children?" Carol asked.

"Now those were cravings," Vivian said. "I remember driving once through most of the night in search of a Baby Ruth."

"I would have given away my right eye for a candy bar," Carol said, laughing.

As the evening faded into twilight, having grown comfortable with silences, Carol noticed the way the blue yellow light filtered through the windows, lying in warm pools over Vivian's bedroom.

"And do you remember that time . . . ?"

"Can you believe both of us . . . ?"

"Can you remember how, with the future fresh in front of us, we used to dream?"

When Vivian tried to respond, she began to cough violently. Carol urged Vivian to rest.

"You are going to need your energy," she said, "to walk down the aisle for Doak's wedding."

As Vivian rested and eventually fell asleep, a realization hit Carol for the first time: Her friend was going to die. After lingering to pray, Carol rose to leave. As she tiptoed out, she heard a soft voice over her shoulder.

"Can you stay a little longer?" Vivian asked. "The foot massage felt so wonderful."

It was the least Carol could do; she believed it to be an honor. During the next hour, Vivian spoke only once to her old and dear friend: "Did I tell you that I *will* be walking down the aisle at Doak's wedding?"

✦ ✦ ✦

On April 1 Marti Garlett, a good friend, transcribed an e-mail for Vivian, which was sent to a community of friends, including an inflammatory breast-cancer support group on the Internet.

> ✉ Subject: For Vivian Felix
>
> Date: April 1, 1999 1:07 PM
>
> I am a close friend of Vivian Felix and am writing to you at her request. She currently is unable to write for herself and has asked me to convey the following information to all of you who have become such close friends and supporters to her during her inflammatory breast-cancer ordeal.
>
> She is currently undergoing whole brain radiation, hoping that it will shrink the cancer, particularly the part pressing on the brain stem. As many of you know, her son Doak is being married on April 10. To prevent facial tattoos, Vivian was fitted with a face mask. She wears it during her daily radiation treatments.
>
> Her trajectory is faster than most—certainly faster than what her doctors had anticipated. Her immediate goal is to

stay physically functional in order to participate in the upcoming wedding. Vivian wants all of you to know that she is
preparing for death and wants to die well. She wants you to
rejoice in the present moment and to make sure your daily
lives are filled with quality and love. She also wants you to
know that what is sustaining her is her very strong faith. She
is at peace with God, who continually reassures her things
work together for the good. Her ability to find the right word
is slowing down, making it difficult for her to express herself
in her usual facile way. Her right hand is becoming immobi-
lized, making it impossible to write. Her eyesight is fading,
making it difficult to read. If nothing changes, you will hear
from me next after her son's wedding on April 10. Even
though it is only 10 days away, it sometimes feels like a
long, even insurmountable span of time.

✦ ✦ ✦

On Easter Sunday—April 4, 1999—Vivian insisted on going to
church. She desired to hear the story of Jesus, who against all odds,
rose from the dead. As Doak and I helped her into a wheelchair,
she looked out over her back porch.

"Did you see the green sprouts already in our garden?" she asked.
I told her I had not noticed.

It was not a coincidence, Vivian believed, that Easter Sunday always fell in spring: from death rises life. The seed dying in good soil
eventually bears a harvest of fruit, and from suffering can rise the
paradox of God's presence. In one of the last letters she wrote—dic-
tated through a friend—Vivian described her thoughts on Easter.

*Henri Nouwen, one of my favorite writers, speaks of Jesus'
agony in the garden of Gethsemane and the events that followed. When our lives are in full swing, before we contemplate that they will indeed come to an end, we think of
ourselves as people of action. When inevitably we fall ill and
face imminent death, we struggle to understand better what it
means to move from action to passion.*

*Jesus' arrest in the garden radically divides his life in two.
The first part is filled with activity, with all sorts of initiatives.
He speaks; he preaches; he heals; he travels. But immediately
after Jesus is handed over, he becomes the one to whom things
are being done. He's being taken before Pilate; he's being
crowned with thorns; he's being nailed on a cross. Things are
being done to him over which he has no control. Nouwen says
that that is the meaning of passion—being the recipient of
other people's initiatives. It involves waiting. For the past
two years, it seemed to me the Lord said, "Wait and be still."
I did not know what that meant. All action ends in passion
because the response to our action is out of our hands.
That is the mystery of work, the mystery of love, the mystery
of friendship, the mystery of community.*

*I am learning that my vocation as a person has not only been
fulfilled by my actions, but by my passion. You, my greater
family, have waited with me as I have learned these eternal
lessons.*

On Easter Sunday, Vivian laid her head on my chest while listening to a sermon by our pastor, Gordon Kirk, about Christ's resurrection, the firstfruit of those who will rise from the dead. When

she found the strength to look up into my eyes, I could see a nearly perfect serenity.

"The resurrection of Jesus," Vivian whispered to me. "That will be done for me."

On one of the days between Easter and Doak's wedding, I sensed a distinct and overwhelming feeling of the presence of the Holy Spirit. Like fog falling in moonlight, the mood of our house possessed the texture of the otherworldly, the mystery of seeing dimly into the unseen. For the last few months, this had not been an unusual experience. In the days, weeks, and months following Vivian's decision to relinquish prayers for healing to me, she had been determined to learn as much as she could.

159

In between bouts of sleep, I understood Vivian to be practicing the spiritual exercises of private prayer, the imprinting of the Word, and heartfelt worship. The further her disease progressed, the more she entered into the healing presence of God. During these times of devotion it would often feel, from an unseen distance, that Vivian had entered into a different spiritual zip code. I could tell by the atmosphere of our house when those times had come.

On one such afternoon, I retreated to my study, down the hall from our bedroom, to pray for her healing. I must confess: My mind wandered. With an increasing sense of disconnectedness, I recalled or imagined single images or thoughts, one against the next against the next. I was like a man who had forgotten the luxury of transitions. I thought about the dream Vivian had before her diagnosis: the tumor that grew and festered and then fell into the ground, and its one single stalk of blood red and beautiful bloom. I remembered the two resolutions she made before coming to California in 1990: to praise God in everything and to hold loosely the things of this world. I recalled her stunning presence in her favorite red dress. In an image of me applying ointment to her ravaged chest, I could hear her words: *Richard, thanks for loving me like this*.

It suddenly occurred to me that even before her battle with cancer, Vivian was being prepared to enroll in the school of dying graces. In 1995, she reread *Foxe's Book of Martyrs* and called it her favorite. During the latter part of 1997 and the first few months of 1998, her journals record notes on her reading from the desert fathers and mothers—their mystical and otherworldly visions. Throughout her battles with cancer, she prayed to God to give her new eyes to see the invisible, underlying, and unrelenting reality of the Kingdom.

My realizations were slowly combined with, and then replaced by, a series of images of Vivian and our life together. Staring out the window onto the street, I was struck by pictures of Vivian before her cancer: The black dress she wore on our first date—the way it fit her shoulders perfectly and brought out the lovely dark hues of her skin and hair. Vivian with Doak, our firstborn, cradled in a blue hospital blanket. Vivian standing on the pier in Shanghai on her fortieth birthday—the same place she had departed at the age of three to come to America. Her smile for Melissa after the second-grade play. Vivian with jewelry reflecting the sun. Vivian near the Gulf of Mexico on our tenth anniversary. Vivian's hand softly on my face. Vivian walking with Tris along silver tide pools. The color of the moon through a gathering fog along Cambria's coast. Her plots to scramble the furniture of a vice president at APU. A station wagon full of children on their way to see *Star Wars* for the first time. The time in Wichita when she put lobster and some salt into the bathtub. The joy of calling Lance, her only daughter's husband, her son. The way her hair used to flow and her body curved.

One after the other, increasing rapidly in sequence, the images came to me—the good times, the wonderful moments—and I lost track of all time. It could have been a few minutes. It could have been a lifetime. Having reached a blur, the images stopped. Once again, I was looking out a window on the street where we lived. Impressed with the need to write down what I had just experienced, I jumped to get my journal and then settled back into the couch. I could not then recollect a single image. It was as if my mind and my memory had been swept clean. I possessed only two seemingly opposing feelings—great loss and great joy.

161

The feeling of joy was greater. By a gift of God's grace, I was reminded of the wonderful life I had with a woman I truly loved. Convinced of my great loss, I remember the surprise of the peace I experienced.

Two days before Doak's wedding, Carol Wagstaff sent an e-mail to a friend urging prayer for Vivian's strength.

 Subject: Wedding Plans
Date: 4/8/99 7:23 PM

Last night I went to the Felixes to take them dinner. All the kids are home for the wedding and more company is coming soon. Vivian is very weak. She was able to talk and make sense but not able to walk much at this point.

She is on steroids to keep the brain lesions down, but they make her muscles very weak. She wants desperately to be able to walk down the aisle. If she goes off the steroids she will be sleeping too much. So it will be touch and go. She has lost her hair again with the last round of chemo, and she has the moon face that comes with taking steroids. I am hoping and praying she will make it through.

Carol

On the day before her son's wedding, Vivian took time to exercise her legs and her faith. She forced herself out of bed for the first time in weeks. With my support, she walked a few steps around our bedroom. When I helped her back into bed, I noticed she was trying not to show the ferocity of her pain.

Our plan for the next day was simple. Tris, who was also Doak's best man, would help Vivian out of the wheelchair and assist her efforts to walk down the aisle. I would follow, prepared to assist my son in carrying Vivian to her seat if she fell.

On April 10, after Stephanie's parents were seated in the church, before Tris had a chance to help, Vivian rose to her feet by herself. Wearing a white mother-of-the-groom dress pinned with a red and white corsage, Vivian held loosely onto her son's arm. She stood firm. Without hesitation or faltering, walking in soft blue light falling through tiers of stained-glass windows, she took a seat of honor for her oldest son's wedding. Those who saw her that day still refer to a strange and graceful radiance.

22 FACING DEATH

In the hope we harbored for her healing, against a terrifying compilation of losses, one reality seemed to defy the sure logic that the Beast would win: Vivian's untouched beauty. It didn't matter if the disease forced her to cover up her scars with a loose-fitting blouse, her baldness with a bandanna, or anemia with a makeup blush, she always managed to possess a beauty beyond comprehension. During the ongoing treatment, if I heard it once, I heard it a hundred times: "She looks like a million bucks."

Our younger son, Tris, was perhaps most vulnerable to confusing his mother's ongoing loveliness for the defiance of persistent health. Unlike our other two children, who were able to see their mother at consistent intervals, Tris could visit only sporadically. Having recently started a job as a lawyer for a firm in Wichita, Kansas, obligations and distance prevented him from coming home as often as he wished. Before each visit, Tris would brace himself for a change in his mother's appearance. And, with each new visit, he could not help but question: *Can a woman who looks so good really be doing as badly as the doctors are suggesting?*

Even as he helped his mother walk down the aisle at his brother's wedding, Tris's focus was on Vivian's underlying radiance. Despite a face pocked from brain radiation and cheeks swollen by steroids, the beauty of her face persisted. If the end was so near, Tris expected a more ravaged and hollowed-out countenance. He, like the rest of us, could be forgiven if he took secret refuge in what he could not see.

On the last weekend in April 1999, high in the Rocky Mountains, Tris arrived for a family meeting planned and organized by his mother. Walking into a rented condominium nestled in breathtaking beauty, Tris could not have prepared himself for what he saw. In the weeks since Doak's wedding, the cancer had ravaged any remaining hint of outward beauty. In addition to the wasting effects of treatment and disease, Vivian had fallen a few days previously. Across her right eye was a gash nearly two inches long, and the entire side of her face was black-and-blue and heavily swollen. When Tris looked his mother in the eyes, he could see only one. Although he tried to protect his mother from any sign of revulsion, Vivian apologized. She had fallen on her way to the bathroom—the muscles of her legs, weakened by medication, had simply given out. Her face had smashed into the corner tiles of the bathtub.

For the first time since the diagnosis of his mother's cancer, Tris understood: He was looking into the face of death.

✦ ✦ ✦

When she requested the attendance of each immediate family member for a weekend in the Rocky Mountains, Vivian did not hint at her overriding purpose. Along with the rest of us, Tris assumed it was to say good-bye and spend what might be our last time together. On the first evening after dinner in the small mountain town of Frisco, Vivian revealed a greater intention: to plan her funeral.

While the rest of us sat stunned, nervously sipping from coffee cups or pulling threads from a sweater, Tris did not hesitate. He walked over to the desk and grabbed paper and pen. To honor his mother's last wishes, he was prepared to overcome his own natural feelings of reticence. In a businesslike manner, Tris faithfully recorded his mother's intentions. In planning her own service and memorial—one for closest family and friends and another for her greater community—Vivian hoped to develop a simple spirit of loving gratitude toward God. Tris promised to make certain her wishes were carried out to the last detail.

The morning after helping plan her funeral, Tris lay down next to his mother in one of the condominium's bedrooms. Through windows overlooking Lake Dillon, they watched a slow fog rising off the waters. The boats of fishermen, backlit by the morning sun, glided on a horizon of pink skies. In a long silence, Vivian reached over and took the hand of her son. She said how proud she was of him. She told him how much it disappointed her that she wouldn't be around to know his wife and her grandchildren.

Even in the face of death, Tris understood his mom was teaching her children. Through a series of one-on-one meetings with each of them, she created opportunities to remove traces of regret. When Vivian was a young woman, her father died in a car accident. It had always bothered her that she wasn't able to say good-bye. In contrast, she wanted to leave this world knowing that she had expressed all that needed to be said to her own children, that all hearts had been unburdened, and that there were no regrets.

Holding hands, watching the sun rise over the lake, they told each other how much they loved one another. Vivian apologized to Tris; she believed she could have been a better mom. Tris said it was he who needed to seek forgiveness. There were times when he felt he had treated her disrespectfully. They asked one another for grace and gave it freely. She would miss him. He would miss her. In contrast to when he had taken notes for her funeral, Tris was emotional. They both wept and laughed. They both expressed pride in each other. They both knew the end was near. They both understood: It might be their last time together.

When their time was over, Tris took a walk alone. In the solitude of the beauty surrounding him, he tried to remember his mother before the cancer. He couldn't. He deeply felt the loss of healthy memories. As he walked along praying to God to see his mother in better days before the Beast, he no longer could recall her past beauty. Whenever he tried to picture her, he could not see past the scars, swelling, and bruises—past the face of death.

In the weeks before my wife died, I too was forced to look into the face of death. After returning home from the Rocky Mountains, Vivian was hospitalized three times to have her lungs drained from an increasingly rapid accumulation of fluids. On the last day of May, after the necessary medical procedures were performed for the final time, I looked into the face of my wife and prayerfully reminded God that the time for a miracle was running out. While I pleaded for God to act, Vivian opened her eyes, grabbed the front of my shirt weakly, and with surprising authority pulled me toward her.

"What are you doing, Richard?" she asked me in her gravelly whisper.

As I looked into the face of death, I could not explain my insistence for a miracle. Before I could respond, she pulled me closer and whispered gently in my ear: "Richard, let me die."

✦ ✦ ✦

On the morning of June 1, 1999, I sent an e-mail to the campus community.

 This has been a very difficult weekend for Vivian, resulting in her having to be hospitalized once again with severe respiratory problems. The cancer is relentless in its onslaught on her poor body. She and I have agreed that now is the time to bring hospice services to our home and this afternoon the hospital has transferred her to our residence on Foxglove.

In addition to sending the e-mail, I called our three children and told them their mother was dying. It was the first time I had said those words.

From the time Tris arrived until the time of his mother's death, he kept a journal.

TUESDAY, JUNE 1, 1999

Rose at 6 AM. drove to KC, flew to Chicago, then to LAX. Doak picked me up; we had a good talk. Mom looked good, somewhat alert, somewhat responsive. We reminisced. I tried to be positive and cheerful. Mom ate a little bit. She really enjoyed a lemon meringue pie Stephanie bought.

Later, Doak played some songs on his guitar and we sang along. We prayed for her, then let her rest.

Dad and I sat and talked about the past and future for a while. He loves her so much and continues to honor her. I love and respect him for that.

Dad slept on the couch next to her all night.

WEDNESDAY, JUNE 2, 1999

Mom looked great this morning. She was smiling and energetic. We had a great morning. She can still use her hands to hold her spoon or glass. She breathes easily with the help of morphine. Mel, Dad, and I went and worked out in the afternoon. It is really good for Dad to release some of the stress.

We visited with Mom some more; she was less alert and seemed tired. We let her rest. We had spaghetti that Doak made for dinner. Mom ate a little. Later, we talked about the memorial services. It was somewhat emotional for Mom. We prayed and let Mom rest for the night.

Melissa slept next to Mom all night. Mom had a difficult breathing episode. My sleep was fitful.

THURSDAY, JUNE 3, 1999

Mom's breathing was much more labored today. She was much more quiet, her voice notably weaker. The morning nurse gave her a quick bath.

Dad & I went to the mortuary. The arrangements were made and I reviewed the paperwork for Dad. It was difficult for him to think and talk about such things, but it is much better to take care of it now than after. I put together a list of people to call with the news upon her passing.

This evening Mom's condition was worse. She could not communicate verbally and could only keep her eyes open for short periods. I turned her oxygen up. We sang a few songs for her and prayed.

FRIDAY, JUNE 4, 1999

I arose early. Mom could open her eyes and use head gestures. It was apparent her condition was deteriorating rapidly. I began a vigil and was soon joined by everyone. We prayed for her, comforted her. I sat or knelt beside her the whole day and night. I cried many tears: for her pain, our loss, and things that could have been. The Lord was a great comfort to me.

About 5:15 PM she lapsed into unconsciousness. She looked around and looked at everyone's face one more time . . . to carry the memory of each one of us with her.

Dad slept on the couch next to her. I sat on the other side of her bed in a chair holding her hand. She still has beautiful hands. By sunrise, she was still with us. Her breathing, although still jerky, had softened.

SATURDAY, JUNE 5, 1999

Vigil continued. Weeping, praying, reading Scriptures, praising.

So tired . . . she refuses to give up. She will not let cancer force her to give up. She has every reasonable excuse to give up, but she continues to be our example. Finish strong. Never give up the good fight. Her spirit and soul will be victorious . . . and ultimately free to join her heavenly Father.

We can't know why Mom was not healed; it is beyond our human capacity to understand. Therefore, we must pray for the strength to remain faithful. It is times like these that test our faith. Thousands of prayers ascended to heaven on Mom's behalf for healing. It never came. But God still blessed us. Mom lived six months beyond doctors' predictions; she was able to celebrate Doak and Stephanie's wedding. This was God's gift to us. Ultimately, God's reward for Mom's unrelenting faith . . . is life everlasting.

JUNE 5, 1999 (CONTINUED)

Mom went into a coma yesterday. She is lying on a hospital bed under her favorite pictures of us kids. The room is so quiet. You only can hear the little noise of oxygen going into her nose. It's peaceful, so peaceful.

*Her body is the only part of her in this world. Her spirit
is with God already.*

*Before she went into a deep sleep yesterday, she
searched for faces. She was so strong mentally and physically. She insisted for a bedpan when she told me she
wanted to go to the bathroom. The nurse told her she
could use the diaper. She refused. She used her strength
to lift her body. We didn't think she could do that but
she had a strong will. That's Mom—so graceful until the
last moment.*

SUNDAY, JUNE 6, 1999

*The vigil continues. . . . Mom's breathing has slowed
some. Continued prayers. A minute never passes that we
aren't holding her hands.*

During his vigil, Tris would not have been able to say how much
time had elapsed since his arrival. The days blurred one into another. Even though he provided comfort, hope, and support for
others, I could see that Tris was isolated—solitary in his grief, loss,
and prayer. Despite extraordinarily beautiful weather, he rarely
went outside. In his nearly around-the-clock attention to his
mother, he prayed often—for relief of his mother's pain, a spirit of
perseverance, and more than anything else, an ability to trade
places with the mother he loved so much. He held her hand almost all the time.

On the morning of June 7, Tris arose and looked out through the
windows of the family room where Vivian lay in her hospice bed. In
the soft angular first light of day, he was struck by a single white
bloom of his mother's rosebush—rising above a mass of crimson

color. Its beauty filled him with an uneasy mixture of love and loss. In a chair by his mother's side, he prayed for her death to be as painless as possible. A few hours later, the hospice nurse and Marsha Fowler—a nurse from APU and one of Vivian's friends—came to clean and change his mother. As he and Melissa walked toward the kitchen together, Tris could hear Vivian's breathing change. In a few minutes, Marsha came to get Tris and Melissa. Sensing panic, I rushed from the bedroom to join my two children at their mother's side.

As I put my hand on his shoulder, Tris held his mother's hand.

With tears in her eyes, Melissa looked at Tris and we understood she could not bear to stay and watch. Long before, Tris had determined to be with his mother at the moment of her death. After a few minutes Vivian gasped for air, and Tris tenderly put his head to her chest. Marsha recorded her vitals. Suddenly, Vivian became still.

In the silence that followed and remained, we all had a sense of another presence in the room; we could not say if it was the Spirit of God or a sweet lingering of Vivian before she passed on. Nearly simultaneously, the presence arrived and the soul of my wife, with the weight of a butterfly carried by the breeze, departed.

✦ ✦ ✦

In the summer of 2000 during a night full of stars, I had a dream of Vivian in the present tense.

I hear the sound of a train in the distance, which is soft as fog lying along the winding path of a green valley. It leaves me thinking of Vivian and wrestling a homesickness. In a station far from where I live, I peer down the tracks at a single white eye rapidly approaching. My children, who are with me, must wonder: *Where is it we are going?*

I ask myself: *What trip do I have planned?*

With the hiss and click of steam brakes, the train stops, and I look up at the moving passengers silhouetted against yellow light the texture of smoke. I feel a vague and unexpected sense of anticipation building in me; I cannot imagine why. For compelling reasons I am unable to explain, I run down the length of the train. My heart pounds within me.

I notice her. Stepping off the train with her red dress on, she turns her head and, with perfect timing, smiles at me with the same smile she always used after we had been apart. As she moves down the steps, I run forward, looking behind for my children, shouting her name. Rising up a step, I reach toward her and notice she has worn my favorite outfit. Simple and elegant, with long flowing sleeves, slightly pleated at the waist, the red dress perfectly accents her figure, which, as before, is full and curving. Against her dark complexion and black hair, her eyes are so alive.

173

"Come," I yell to my children, "your mother has returned."

I turn around to hear my daughter tell me, "Dad, we have a trip to go on."

I climb another step, and as I reach out to take hold of my wife, the dream ends.

I awake to another day without Vivian, confident in the hope I will one day see her again.

23 VISIONS OF HOPE

How long, O Lord?
Will you forget me forever?
How long will you hide your face from me?
How long must I wrestle with my thoughts and
every day have sorrow in my heart?
How long will my enemy triumph over me?

Look on me and answer, O Lord my God.
Give light to my eyes,
or I will sleep in death; my enemy will say,
"I have overcome him,"
and my foes will rejoice when I fall.

But I trust in your unfailing love;
my heart rejoices in your salvation.
I will sing to the Lord,
for he has been good to me.
—*Psalm 13*

During a season of restlessness in the fall of 1996, my wife looked out over the Avon River, which had inspired Shakespeare, and found her focus shifting. On the grounds of England's Warwick Castle, seeking a higher perspective, Vivian had climbed a mound in search of a place to pray.

From the spot where she was sitting, on the campus of a fortress established by William the Conqueror, she wondered how many battles had been fought, how much blood spilled, how many intrigues seeded. She imagined the conquests celebrated, losses mourned, kings crowned, and heads lost. Just miles downstream in Stratford, Shakespeare had once penned a plea from Warwick.

> *Clifford of Cumberland, 'tis Warwick calls:*
> *And if thou dost not hide thee from the bear,*
> *Now, when the angry trumpet sounds alarum*
> *And dead men's cries do fill the empty air,*
> *Clifford, I say, come forth and fight with me:*
> *Proud northern lord, Clifford of Cumberland,*
> *Warwick is hoarse with calling thee to arms.* *

In Vivian's mind, from a higher perspective, a larger picture was emerging. The words of the Great Bard and the wars of Great Britain: From just one pen and one country had the world ever been so changed? In many ways, Vivian understood she was on top of the world. While praying, she experienced an epiphany—an even higher and greater perspective.

> *I could look over it all, see it from the top—almost as if*
> *I was seeing it from the eyes and perspective of God himself.*

*From *King Henry VI*, part 2, act 5, scene 2

*I saw the veil lifted between my world as I see it and the
reality of the world filled with God's goodness, grace, and
love. And what I saw was a whole world—an entire
world—that sparkles with the Light of God; that everything holds together, has its life, and is sustained and
blessed by the grace of God.*

After the diagnosis of her breast cancer, Vivian defined those
moments high above the river Avon as critical to finding her way.
As the regulated poison of chemotherapy dripped into her blood
just a few months later, she wrote:

177

*The experience I had in England as I stood on the
mound built by William the Conqueror was given to me
as a grace and precursor to my cancer. It was as if I had
stepped into another plane of existence and the scales
fell from my eyes. I knew then I had never seen the
world as it really is, because this is how it really is.
A great and sudden joy and peace filled me as I knew
everything was in God's hands and all will work for
his good purposes.*

*As I looked over the beautiful English countryside
with the ancient trees and gentle river, I knew that
God is goodness and light and that I needed to live
in that knowledge and assurance. From this experience,
I understood that all my life is his and he is working
to bring me into a full relationship with him.
Everything is a grace and this year with cancer is
a gift to me.*

Throughout the journals chronicling her losing war to a dark and terrible disease, she referred back, like a carpenter with a level or a sea captain a compass, to a moment when the veil had ripped.

I praise you, Father of Light, for sending a light to me—
for allowing me for a moment to see with the eyes
of faith.

I am by no means a mystic. That was Vivian's spiritual territory. She was the one to see visions, hear God calling, and explore the spiritual metaphors she believed to be whispering of the greater and invisible reality of God's Kingdom. I am given over to pragmatism and more tangible realities. Before the events surrounding my wife's cancer, I had never even remotely experienced a vision, dream, or spiritual trance. And if I had, I probably would have been too embarrassed to admit it.

178

In the wake of my wife's death, I will freely admit to a few experiences that I cannot explain and, having ruled out other causes, I attribute only as gifts from God in the form of healing grace.

✦ ✦ ✦

A few weeks after her death, restless with memories of Vivian, I got in my car and drove to the Salt Creek Beach. For the first time since we sold our condominium, I returned to the ocean. The beach was nearly deserted. It was unusually cold and windy for July, and I wished I had brought a jacket with me. I looked out over the churning surf through tears in my eyes, unsure whether it was the breeze or the memories stinging me. In the distance I saw the sails of boats filled with the speed of racing wind pushing them to-

ward the horizon. I opened my Bible and read Psalm 71:19-21, one
of Vivian's favorite passages.

> Your righteousness reaches to the skies, O God,
> you who have done great things.
> Who, O God, is like you?
> Though you have made me see
>   troubles, many and bitter,
> you will restore my life again;
> from the depths of the earth
> you will again bring me up.
> You will increase my honor
> and comfort me once again.

179

Before I realized it, my mind settled on the image of me sitting
under a full mast, washed by sea and salt, growing smaller and
smaller, and finally disappearing. Over the horizon, I prayed I
would see Vivian. Stung by the cold, I hunched over a Bible and
closed my eyes; the fury of the wind and the water was somehow as
full of sorrow as rage—the cry of a world broken and without
meaning. I don't know how long I listened to the howling before a
vision arose. Having sailed over the edge of the world, weeping
over inevitable losses, I saw myself look up, and there before me,
approaching silently and rapidly, was Vivian. Without boundary
or backdrop, sea or sky, my sailboat was gone and I was walking in a
bright white light one could imagine heaven to be filled with. It
was as soft as it was startling. A chill danced along my heart and
warmed me. When we embraced, I felt as if I had made it home.

Like a child, Vivian always radiated a high-beam smile in the presence of surprise. I will never forget the look on her face as she pulled back to look at me and say how missed I had been. The white light seemed to be falling, pooling, cleansing, and finally gathering. Vivian and I, hand in hand, turned to face the source of the light—a man standing before us. As hard as we tried, we could not look up into his face; the light dazzled and shook us. At the same time, we dropped to our knees and could not separate our fear from our gratitude. As the man held out his hand to us, he spoke softly, but like the roaring of a thousand voices on a wind-ravaged sea. To Vivian, the Voice said: "My child, you lived this wonderful life, you suffered this horrible disease, and you remained faithful to me. Because of this, your children will be with you in heaven." From pure joy, the tears were streaming down both of our faces. When the man turned toward me, the bright light was brighter, comfortably blinding, and he told me that I, too, had held on to faith: "You will see your grandchildren in heaven." Just as I reached out to touch his hand, I woke up shivering, huddled over against a cold wind. My Bible was stained with tears. Against the biting edge of the wind, I walked to my car and drove home.

✦ ✦ ✦

One month short of the second anniversary of Vivian's death, I was visiting the Garden Isle of Kauai, planning a Sunday of prayer and meditation somewhere in the mountains where the temperatures would be cooler. I decided to make the drive to the western shore and then proceed to the top of Waimea Canyon, the one that Mark Twain called the Grand Canyon of the Hawaiian Islands.

The drive from Poipu Beach along the western shore is quite

beautiful. After passing through Kalaheo, the road winds through coffee plantations and then the tall fields of sugar cane. All the while the blue Pacific Ocean beckons for your attention. Finally I arrived at the little town of Waimea at the sea's edge. This remote town is almost pure Hawaiian with only a little commercialization evident downtown.

By midmorning the heat was already in the low eighties. I headed up a steep ascent on the paved road to the canyon—a series of hairpin curves that provides a ribbon effect to drivers. Within a mile I passed a small group of homes on a mesa with wonderful views of the Pacific Ocean and the remote island of Niihau. Thinking of the more spectacular views higher on the mountain, I remembered that many people often settle for the first beautiful thing that God gives them and miss other opportunities that may be awaiting them.

After about three miles I pulled off the road to take a more complete view of the seascape that I had left behind. The temperature had dropped several degrees, and the gentle sea breeze wafted a fragrance of peace and release. I used this time to pray for my family and friends, grateful for this unique setting as a catalyst for easy praying and listening.

Within a few minutes I realized a major cloud formation was reducing my available sunlight, and the wind was whistling through my car window, slightly rolled down. Condensation began forming on my windshield, necessitating an occasional reach for the wiper control.

After I'd begun to drive again, I realized that the clouds were touching and covering the trees alongside the road. Patches of clouds and fog began to cover the road, forcing almost a complete slowdown of my rental car. Cars were now pulled over to the side of the road and oncoming cars with headlights at full beam were crawling like snails down the hill. I felt as if I had entered another world.

Finally, I reached Kokee State Park. Socked in the cloud cover, dozens and dozens of motorists had taken refuge in its huge parking lot and were making use of the dining and shopping facilities. A nearby sign read, Kelalau Lookout Point: Three Miles.

I am not sure why I continued driving on, except that morning I had had a vision of praying at the top of the canyon with vistas of ocean to pray over. The cloud cover was now so soupy that condensation gathered on everything. It was then that I imagined the presence of angels. My mind began to envision the clouds as a heavenly transportation system for angels. Of course, I realized that formless angels do not need clouds, which have form, in order to move about the unseen heavenly universe. But the thought of angels moving in groups among the clouds continued to occupy my consciousness.

I was driving very slowly, encountering only one car heading down the hill from the lookout point. Surrounded by clouds, fog, mist, and condensation, I finally parked my car in one of the vacant spaces at the lookout. I couldn't see anything around me, not even the trees or the lookout point, only the soupy cloud cover. I became aware of the wind and moisture trying to force their way through the small crack of window. The next thing I remember is the window rolling down a few inches farther and a powerful gust of wind coming through, brushing my face and resounding with an echo for several seconds inside the car.

It seemed that I was in some kind of dream state. I heard a voice. It was Vivian, saying, "You knew it was me, didn't you?" In my dream I nodded yes without saying a word. I can only recall that her presence was smiling; I did not see her. I didn't even glance in the direction of her voice, because I knew there would be no bodily form, just a smiling countenance.

I proceeded to tell her all about what was happening in my life, what each of the children was doing, that Melissa and Lance had given her a little granddaughter, that Tris was now happily married and his wife was expecting a baby boy in June. I continued to sense just a peaceful, smiling presence.

I told her how much she was missed by her family . . . that we all loved her dearly and missed her at Tris's wedding . . . that I had lit a candle in her honor at the front of the church . . . that no doubt she was there during the whole ceremony.

183

Only a smiling countenance.

Finally, I realized I was crying, telling her how much I loved and missed her.

She spoke: "Richard, where I journey to and from there are no tears."

Then she added, "Remember there are thousands and thousands of angels at your beck and call at any time."

Finally, she said, "Tell the children to stay close to Jesus." All the time my head was bowed, and I only nodded in agreement when she spoke.

I awoke from the dream with my shirt, shorts, and steering wheel covered with condensation. The window had remained rolled down the whole time. I also realized the engine was still running, because I had failed to turn it off earlier when I placed the gearshift in park. I quickly rolled up the window and turned off the engine.

Searching for something to dry myself off with, I found a few napkins along with a ballpoint pen. I began to write down the elements of the dream on the back of a realtor's sales sheet.

Then I sat there for quite a while savoring the experience, wondering if angels really do travel in cloud formations. Maybe *Vivian* traveled in the clouds with angels. I was smiling as I wiped away the tears that just wouldn't stop flowing. How could a person be so happy and so sad at the same time?

I peered out my window and could faintly see the lookout point in the distance. I knew I wanted to go pray at the point, even more so now than ever. I left my car and began the short walk to the chain-link fence that kept people from the edge of the ocean cliff.

On my right side, no more than ten feet away, was a woman doing tai chi. She was tanned, almost bronze, with long straight hair that fell down her back below her waistline. Her movements were flawless and effortless. I sneaked a glance and she was smiling at me. I offered a weak smile in return and continued to the lookout point. I could not see the blue ocean below and beyond because of the clouds and misty air.

I noticed to my left an Asian man, half sitting on a bicycle and half leaning on the chain-link fence. He was staring straight ahead into the clouds. I inched slowly in his direction and thought I might engage him in conversation. When he glanced over and saw me coming he returned his stare toward the cloudy abyss and began to speak.

"A most beautiful day. Perfect in every way. Up here there is no ceiling, no floor, no walls—only the small place where we stand." He paused for a moment. I said nothing.

Then he began again. "The southern and southeasterly winds are blowing this way. Going to keep it this way for few more hours at least. I love it like this. Nothing is in this place, yet everything is in this place. When I look all around me it makes me want to fly out into that world and explore it to its fullest. Wouldn't you like to do that?"

Half-mesmerized by his words, I stood there nodding my head yes while peering deeply into the surrounding clouds. Sensing my silence, he turned and looked at me briefly. "Yes, sir," I spoke, "it surely does." He turned back to his thoughts.

I returned to my car, passing the woman who was still doing her tai chi. She smiled at me again. The beads of condensation on her cheeks and forehead added to her overall beauty.

I drove slowly through the soup back to Kokee State Park, trying to soak in all that had just happened. Looking back, I noticed the Asian man had walked over to where the woman was doing tai chi. They seemed to be talking to each other, but she never stopped her movements. I pulled off into a parking lot to write it all down, then continued back down the canyon.

Driving became easier and easier as I left the cloud cover behind. When I reached bottom I paused to look back to the top of Waimea Canyon. *The clouds are still there.* Perhaps it was an assurance from my beloved Bringer of Hope that we do indeed live on earth among the presence of angels, and Jesus is closer to us than we can possibly know.

Vivian had asked God for a new ministry, and only through the school of dying graces could that prayer be answered. Vivian learned in dying what I believe we all need for living. In this earthly life, we are offered holy ground on which to walk. And we have the opportunity to do so with grace upon grace.

185

"Lord, make me beautiful
of soul, and then let others
see into my soul. . . . Expand
my life outward, Lord. Let
my life have ultimate meaning.
Allow me to bring hope and
your love to others."

–From the journal
of Vivian Felix

Richard and Vivian Felix